THE HAND OF GOD

THE HAND OF GOD!

GOD UNSEEN HANDS IN OUR LIFE JOURNEY

By

BOSE WILLIAMS FOR RECONCILIATION MINISTRIES

XULON PRESS

Xulon Press
2301 Lucien Way #415
Maitland, FL 32751
407.339.4217
www.xulonpress.com

© 2022 by Bose Williams for Reconciliation Ministries

All rights reserved solely by the author. The author guarantees all contents are original and do not infringe upon the legal rights of any other person or work. No part of this book may be reproduced, stored in a retrievable system, or transmitted in any form or by any means without the prior written permission of the author.

Due to the changing nature of the Internet, if there are any web addresses, links, or URLs included in this manuscript, these may have been altered and may no longer be accessible. The views and opinions shared in this book belong solely to the author and do not necessarily reflect those of the publisher. The publisher therefore disclaims responsibility for the views or opinions expressed within the work.

Unless otherwise indicated, Scripture quotations taken from the New King James Version (NKJV). Copyright © 1982 by Thomas Nelson, Inc. Used by permission. All rights reserved.

Paperback ISBN-13: 978-1-6628-5377-7
Hard Cover ISBN-13: 978-1-6628-5378-4
Ebook ISBN-13: 978-1-6628-5379-1

Table of Content

Introduction ix
Chapter One – In the Beginning 1
Chapter Two – The early days. 7
Chapter Three – Divine Timing. 21
Chapter Four – Taking the Bull by the Horn 31
Chapter Five – My Dysfunctional Family. 51
Chapter Six – Experience versus Head Knowledge. 59
Chapter Seven – My School Years – St. Dominic 69
Chapter Eight – The Crux of the matter 97
Chapter Nine – The Heart – the Hub 137
Chapter Ten – No pain, no gain. 163
Chapter Eleven – Habit #1 – Confronting guilt. 169
Chapter Twelve – Habit #2 – Confronting Anger 185
Chapter Thirteen – Habit #3 – Confronting Greed. 213
Chapter Fourteen – Habit #4 – Confronting Jealousy . . . 233
Chapter Fifteen – Charity Begins at Home. 261
Epilogue. 263

Introduction

Chance or Providence?

All through the bible, both in the New and Old Testaments, we see how frequently God's providence is so clearly displayed, sometimes within layers or clouds of disguise. Many times, we assume that nothing is happening to us when things seem to stagnate, but the unseen hand of God, his hands of providence is always at work on our behalf. He is all the time shifting and re-arranging things, times and seasons so that his plan for us will manifest.

"My ways are not your ways and my thoughts are not your thought," says the Lord, and these eternal words are confirmed by Jeremiah 10:27 which says "I know the thought that I think towards you, thought of good and not evil to give you an expected end and a future you deserve".

This scripture explains how God works behind the scenes to bring his purpose for our lives to come to pass. When God uses some extreme measures in our life we tend, as humans, to assume we ought to intuitively figure it out. We don't give our full attention to seeing or understanding the providential direction God wants us to take at this particular season, circumstance, or event. This invariably leads us to ignorantly disobey God or take the wrong route. Yes, the wrong route which at that time looks, seems, or, feels humanly right. In some cases, we rubber-stamp our actions and justify them with a good "churchy" cliché particularly when we are amid other "churchy" folks. While doing so, the Holy Spirit's voice is ignored, drowned out, or not silenced by being quenched or grieved. What happens next is that we run into stormy water and begin to blame God, our family members, friends, and even the government.

From the time we are planted in our mother's womb and throughout our lifespan, God's providence can be seen if we are careful to observe situations and circumstances because there is always a script being played out. Have you ever thought about why you were born into a particular Country, State, City, Family, or Race, or why you were born at such a time as this? Or do you feel like everything and everybody is against you or that you are holding the wrong end of the stick in life?

It is usual for us to ascribe all of these to chance or coincidence. But, God in His infinite wisdom made it impossible for us among other things beyond our control to determine which family or race, or country we would be born into. In other words, our origin is by divine choice and not by chance. If this is so, doesn't it stand to reason that we are playing a script written by the great hand of providence?

In this book I have tried to share my story and to show how the hand of God was at work and is still at work in my life to prove just one point – no one is here on planet earth by accident! We are all part of the master plan of the great weaver. Reading my story may give the impression that I am a child of circumstance and that perhaps if the circumstances surrounding my birth and upbringing had been different, my story may have also been different. I do not have all the answers but I am convinced that my life testimony is the story of providence and divine arrangement.

It was my mother who told me the details of my birth and looking back on all that I have experienced and gone through, I am glad the choice was not left to me. From an early age, I despised the very family I was born into, even more so after my mother told me about her own experience before I was born. I came to detest who I was and was overcome with shame and guilt, two enemies that fought against the realization of my destiny and kept me from living the life God created me to live but thanks be to God I found the truth that has liberated me and I want to share the story of my journey through life with you knowing that you too will be set free.

God bless you!

Bose

Chapter One

In the Beginning!

My mother was the third of my dad's three wives, which meant that my mother had to compete with the other two wives to get my dad's attention. This often resulted in the other two wives teaming up together to bully my mother. Even though they never saw eye to eye, my mother became their common enemy, just like Festus and Herod became friends to condemn Jesus in the Gospel. I am the second child of six siblings and the first daughter of my mother, but I am the tenth child and the fifth daughter of my dad.

The age difference between my mother and my two step-mothers worsened the situation for my mother because culturally she was not supposed to talk back to either of them. Sometimes physical abuse was involved, particularly from the older stepmother. The abuse ranged from slapping my mother, spitting on her, or pouring dirty dishwater on her while my mother just looked on. I watched as the older stepmother tore my mother's clothes and yet my mother wouldn't say a word, instead, she would sit crying as my older brother and I looked on crying along with her and for her.

From an early age, I was not happy and had a lot of questions but did not know how to express them or search for answers. My mother would talk to me as though I understood our situation. Looking back at those days I realize that such conversations bonded me with my mother. Even as I grew up, I became her best friend and confidant. This experience taught me to be a good listener at an early age because I could not interrupt but just sit and listen to my mother talk. In between sobs, she would interject with spontaneous praises and thanks to God, as she pulled me into her arms and prayed over me. I would be confused about the mixture of emotions that I was witnessing. On several occasions, while my mother was going through these emotions, my older stepmother would angrily stomp in front of her, mocking and using words that I later understood to be cursing. When she saw that my mother kept on singing, she proceeded to physical abuse.

My dad worked in the carpentry department of the Nigerian Railway Corporation. He was always gone during the day and came home after 5 pm from Monday to Friday. The only time my mother got a break from any abuse was on Saturdays and Sundays when my dad was at home. You would think the house would be quiet while dad was home, but it was far from it. My older stepmother would direct all her anger at my dad which sometimes caused him to physically beat my stepmother. All that anger would be transferred to my mother come Monday morning.

Some days my mother would take my brother and me and just leave the house as soon as my dad was gone. We would l stay out all day which meant hunger, thirst, and sunburn.

The societal status for women was unlike what it is today because in those days women were generally full-time housewives; and home keepers. Some wives were permitted however by their husbands to engage in petty trade when the children were grown. This is usually done right in front of the house or a walking distance and at a general assembly of traders called the 'market.' While the husbands were fully responsible for household upkeep financially, the little money the woman made was nothing to reckon with, so this kept the woman under the spell and control of the man. Women were considered property and are not encouraged to attend school. Since marriages were arranged between parents it was the groom's parents that would look for a suitable wife for their son from any family of their choice as early as 18 -20 years of age. 20 years was considered late for the male while for the girl at an early age of 12 she would be arranged for marriage.

Virginity was a highly coveted virtue for both families, particularly the bride's family. The whole community would celebrate with the bride and her family on the day she is circumcised, usually, in her husband's house and it was not uncommon for most girls to start their menstruation in their husband's house. Sadly, polygamy was well-practiced and endorsed during my mother's early age.

14th Years Before

But this was not the beginning of my mother's saga. The physical, verbal and mental abuse she suffered at the hands of my stepmothers was another story compared to her earlier experience. Some 14 years before becoming my dad's wife; that is at the age of 12 she had been betrothed to a local chief known as Odedegbe an influential man in her community. At that time, he already had 6 other wives and was 56 years old when he married my mother as his seventh wife. He was considered wealthy because he owned a lot of land and a herd of cows. He was also a local herbalist and a fortune teller, thus he was popular and much sort after in his community. Marrying such a man of influence was considered to be a 'blessing' and honor to my mother's parents, who gained land, herds of cows, and recognition as a result.

As the 7th wife and the youngest wife, she was lavished with gold, and money and had maids and servants assigned to her.

Fourteen years passed and my mother could not have a child. As despair and shame set in she began to think of other options. During this period of childlessness, my mother said she went through all sorts of humiliations and was subjected to horrible rituals such as eating the stool of a newborn child, and collecting and drinking the urine of a newborn child. Unfortunately, in those days all childlessness was attributed to the woman never the man. Her only saving grace was that she was still a virgin when she got married.

Life saver- my aunt

One day when my mum's older sister (my aunt) visited, my mother, was for the first time confronted with what she never knew. She was told that for her to get pregnant, her husband must be able to have sexual intercourse with her. According to my mother, after that she was given some concoctions to drink each night which made her dead asleep and so couldn't recall whether her husband was performing his conjugal duties. Unbeknown to her, the local chief was having serious medical issues. He was Diabetic, with long-term complications like erectile dysfunction, and low sperm count.

Now, what is the relevance of this interjection? It is because I want you to see that though there are levels of darkness that come with not knowing God, the good news is that God knows all about us and through his divine providence reveals his plan, allows His purpose to be fulfilled in His time and season.

THE HAND OF GOD

Even in the story of Sarah and Haggai, we saw how the divine providence of God played out as we never read where Haggai called on the name of the living God. She was an Egyptian slave girl, yet something in her heard the voice of the providential God who created her.

Chapter Two

The early days

Enter Mr. Williams (My Father)

My father, Mr. Williams was the only living child of his mother who had lost two other children. His mother was the first of four wives by his dad. At a very young age of 14, my dad met a German man Mr. Jack who was at the time working with a road construction company. Every day after school my dad would go spend the rest of the evening with Mr. Jack, who took an interest in my dad. After 4 years as the road work was being completed, my dad had turned 18. So he left with Mr. Jack to go to the city of Lagos. There he served and stayed with Mr. Jack until he was about to return to Germany which made him help my dad get employed with the Nigerian Railroad Corporation, where my dad until he retired.

Enter Mr. Pius (My maternal Uncle)

My Uncle, Mr. Pius is the third of five siblings. After college, he became employed by the same Nigerian Railroad Corporation in the city of Lagos, and specifically in the same Coach Construction Department as my dad, Mr. Williams.

My dad and my uncle were both from the same state but not from the same city which was a perfect providential setup for what was about to unfold.

On one fateful day, my mother decided to leave her marriage to the local Chief Ogedengbe, forsaking the money and fame. It was a bold and risky move because the local chief was influential and stigmatization that comes with abandoning one's matrimonial home. The only place she knew or felt safe going to was her brother's place, who was shocked and afraid for his life when my mother showed up at his doorstep in faraway Lagos.

As the saying goes blood is thicker than water. So when he saw his sister my mum, he had mixed emotions of fear and the pressure of protecting his sister, especially when she made it clear that she would rather commit suicide than be taken back to the local chief, her current husband.

Staying in his place was not safe for either of them but as providence would have it, they had a 7-day window to hatch a plan before any news of her whereabouts would reach the village. Before the messengers sent by the Chief to look for her would be able to arrive in Lagos, she had to find a safe hiding place. She also had to ensure no one sees or recognizes her so that news of her where about doesn't filter the village. Since there were people from her village living in Lagos it was imperative my mother not be seen by anyone that could recognize her.

The Taxi Driver

My mother's "escape" from the village was also providential. My mother with other passengers from her village took a taxi to the city of Lagos where my maternal uncle Pius resides without any incident. No passenger in the taxi that day knew my mother or the reason for her leaving town. So when the taxi driver made it back to the village an extraordinarily strong message was waiting for him. The local chief had summoned him to his palace, which meant something was wrong. By this time the news had spread that the local chief's youngest wife (my mother) was missing and was last seen in his taxi. During the interrogation of the taxi driver, my mother's parents had to respond immediately to rescue the taxi driver as a co-conspirator. He immediately told them he would gladly take them to the address where he took my mother, which was her brother's house (Pius) who lived within the Nigerian Railways Housing Estate at the time in the city of Lagos.

For the driver's next trip to Lagos, he was charged not to carry any other passengers except six men sent by the local chief selected to go bring my mom back. These six men were instructed to search all the homes of those from the same village where my mother might be hiding. This was supposed to be an easy task because all those from the same village as my uncle Pius attend monthly meetings. They interact with each other as brothers and sisters and everyone knows each other. These six men, sent by the local chief, were instructed to call for an emergency meeting to tell the people the consequence of complicacy in my mother's escape from the local chief.

With the above looming in the heart of my mother's brother, he came up with what could only be a providential plan. Mr. Williams (my to-be father at that time) was not from the same village as my uncle, therefore they would not search his house or even consider him a conspirator.

They also live on opposite sides of the city, extremely far from each other, and only meet at work.

My uncle approached my dad, Mr. Williams, at work and told him about the daring situation. As providence would have it my dad's second wife traveled to his village to have her 5th child. My dad was living alone at that time. Two days before the arrival of the messengers from the local chief, my mother moved in with my dad to escape been taking back to the village. These men would stay till the next market day before they can travel back (spending 7 days in Lagos).

The news of these men's arrival spread like wide fire as they began to physically search the homes of all the men and women who were from the same village as the local chief. Some even got notes from their relatives from home warning them not to participate in the escape of my mother. As days progressed into weeks my mother dared not go back to her brother's house because he had become a prime suspect. The good thing was that there were no phones at that time and the only means of communication were in person, letters, or telegram.

So from Monday to Friday at work, my dad would give my uncle reports about my mother's welfare as she hid in his house.

As weeks progress into months my mother told my dad of the 14 years ordeal of her arranged marriage to a local chief. My mother continuously reminded my dad that any attempt to send her back would result in her taking her life. Back then words are binding, unlike today where a man's words mean nothing. I thank God His words are still as binding in life as they are in Spirit. Mr. Williams (my dad) knew this "woman" talking to him was not joking and he did not want to be the last person to refuse to help her live. Having spent a great deal of time with Mr. Jack, the German man, my dad knew what awaited my mom if she was taken back to the village – exile from her village and life of humiliation, mockery, isolation for her family, and even death. So he was willing to take the risk. As he recalled how Mr. Jack took the risk of helping him, he felt a strong obligation to help my mum whatever it would take.

This custom of reciprocal help was practiced in my dad's village, again the providential hand of God and His divine purpose was strong, persuading him not to give in. Having my mother living with him was not easy, as he had to keep watch over who came or who was watching. Even harder for him was that she had to stay out of sight completely. Their lives were turned upside down! My dad had to do activities outside of his apartment for my mom like fetching water from the public tap, cooking, and washing her clothes. She had to discreetly wash them and would not spread them to dry outside in the sun, which was the usual thing to do. My mother told me she had to wash one set at a time so it could dry overnight.

My Father's Village

After the seven days had passed and the messengers traveled back, the news had spread to the neighboring villages including my dad's. The local chief in dad's village, in solidarity with his colleague Chief Ogedengbe, sent messengers to deliver a message that no one from his village must harbor or take part in aiding my mother's escape from her marriage to the local chief and he enumerated the consequence of such actions. With such a small population, news by words of mouth was a very effective way of communication, particularly one that was against their cultural norm, or something never heard of before.

My Maternal Village Women

Unlike the men in both my maternal and paternal villages, who were united in the opinion that what my mother did was disgraceful and unacceptable, it was a different situation for the women. Though divided in their opinion, the matter was a well-talked-about topic, and one that most of them could relate to and were sympathetic to. There were many ordeals women were subjected to because they could not bear children. My mother remembered how she drank a newborn child's urine, scoop the newborn's stool in her mouth as so call remedies to her barrenness, and how she could not participate in many women's activities as she was virtually a "persona non grata" because she was acclaimed barren. Things were more humiliating for my mother because women younger than her were having their kids and she couldn't. She became an outcast sort! Although my mother said the other wives of the local chief did not have anything bad or evil to say about her condition; as those who were bold enough to utter anything prayed for her while the others kept such good wishes to themselves. What heightened their confusion and unanswered questions was the fact that my mother was a virgin when she got married to the local chief at the young age of 16 and she was publicly circumcised. This brought great relief and was a face-saver to my mother's family. Had this not been the case, it only stands to our imagination what kind of embarrassment and humiliation her escape would have caused the family.

As I explained earlier all barrenness was believed to be due to problems with the women, but never the men. Barrenness was also attributed to some form of witchcraft, curses, or voodoo.

It is never a Male Problem

Erectile dysfunction (ED) was never considered a cause of barrenness because it was reasoned that since older men could get women pregnant, barrenness must be a problem with the woman. This makes those men who have ED believe that they are not the cause of their wives not being able to get pregnant. This was particularly so if the man already had other children before marrying the "barren" wife. The first suspicion in the case of any woman's barrenness was witchcraft. The barren woman would be accused of "eating up her fetus" before they were born, and she will be subjected to swear and take an oath by the gods or deity to prove she was innocent. No male was ever subjected to such "ordeal" and sadly, my mother had her share of this several times as the years progressed.

As a precaution, the other wives of the local chief were made to swear and take an oath that they were not responsible for my mother's barrenness due to jealousy or envy.

Animal Sacrifice and Rituals

My mother made countless sacrifices almost every day to some angry deities or gods of her forefathers, several generations removed. These sacrifices were to appease the gods for all the sins and mistakes she made in her previous life since the people believed in reincarnation.

The Herbalist, fortune tellers, or Seers as they are called interpreted the so-called claims of the gods or deities. They also claimed to be able to identify who the person was in his or her previous lives. In my mother's case, the herbalist told her she had 7 pregnancies and all died in her womb because she apparently 'ate them' in her past life. Even the only one that made it to birth, she refused to breastfeed. She was said to pretend to be ill until the baby died of starvation. Furthermore, she was told she was not a good mother, and that she was cruel to her past husband who died early hence the gods made her marry someone strong enough to subdue her- the local chief who was a renowned herbalist.

With all this information locked up in my mother's heart, she went out of her way to do good deeds with the resolve to restitute for all the evil she may have done in her previous life. As a result of her actions, it was concluded by both men and women in the community that she had repented and changed to be a good person in her lifetime. Praise God that the generous and giving spirit was very much alive as I watched my mother growing up and going out of her way to help and bless others. Sometimes her kind acts were at her inconvenience and discomfort. This was a trait I cherished and wish to carry on in my own life. Being a believer it is imperative for me to also leave the same legacy for my children.

Knowledge is Power

I used to believe that what I do not know can't hurt me. Now I beg to recant such a statement because what I do not know can hurt me. We see the same scenario played out in the bible when God planned that He wanted Adam and Eve to only know that which had no evil. The narrative of the two trees in the garden displays God's plan: the tree of life and the tree of knowledge of good and evil. It suffices to say that Adam and Eve not knowing that God was not hiding anything from them, were convinced by Satan to have a wrong presumption about God and this we still do today. But God is loving and caring. Had they known that God had their best interest at heart they would never have rebelled against his command!

Being completely ignorant of what it takes to get pregnant kept my mother in darkness and wrongly labeled as being barren and childless for a long time. What she didn't know kept her in darkness; made her face unprintable humiliation and heartaches for 14 long years.

The early days

Understanding gives Insightful Authority

In my local dialect, it is said that when a person wakes up from sleep, that becomes his morning! In hindsight, my mother wished her sister had visited and helped her earlier on in her marriage. She was confused in the early years of her marriage and because her husband the local Chief could not have sexual intimacy with her made it all the more confusing. She recalls that she was advised that the first few sexual experiences with her husband would be unpleasant since she was a virgin and circumcised. So she kept wondering when such an experience would come but it never came!

Wisdom! The application of both Knowledge and Understanding

26 years of age was considered a mature age in my mother's days. She could have had 12 children by now, but behold she had none. She had never been pregnant to talk more of giving birth to a child. Now armed with the knowledge from her sister, she confronted her husband one of those nights while he was mixing the usual concoction for her to drink, and boldly asked him why she had not experienced the pain of being dis-flowered, an experience that she was cautioned about on the day of her circumcision.

This was not a question her husband had ever expected from her since none of his other wives was bold enough to ask him. He told my mother she probably had already forgotten because she was always asleep when she came to spend the night with him. According to traditional beliefs, no woman came to the local chief's chambers during her 5-day or so menstrual period and an extra 3 days after due to ritual cleansing. Also on days that the local chief is undergoing spiritual consecration or days demanded by the gods for him to observe abstinence, no woman was permitted to come near him.

After that fateful day that my mother asked the unexpected question, her husband drastically limited the days she could sleep in his chambers. For some months, she will not be invited to sleep in her husband's chamber at all. Knowing that she could not confront him because she would be seen as not being cooperative with the god's demands, she decided to swallow her disappointment and seek a solution herself. It would have been a worse ordeal for her if she had exposed her husband because it was held that it is the gods that enabled women to be pregnant and also enabled people to get a great harvest, plenty of rain, and protection from illness and evil.

If I die, I die

One fateful day my mother decided she has had enough; if she was to die then so be it but she was

The early days

determined to do something. She made the unprecedented and unheard-of move to escape from her 14 years of ordeal once and for all. She refused to let the fear of being caught paralyze or keep her in such bondage, prison, and falsehood any longer.

What also fueled her resolve was the unceremonious burial of a barren woman that she had witnessed and it was something she dreaded. No one was allowed to shed tears of mourning for the barren woman since it was believed that her condition was a curse from the gods. Worse still the parents of the dead childless woman were forbidden to attend the burial or even mourn. Her remains were not allowed to stay overnight in the house as she must be buried the same day no matter the time of her death and on a designated plot of land separate from the burial place reserved for her family. These were some of the fear that my mother and her family lived with every day for 14 years.

Accordingly, a plot of land is given to every child in the family and that is where they were to be buried by the surviving children so in the case of my mother her plot of land given to her by her father will be automatically given to her parents' first grandchild from my mother's side as she would be buried in what is called "the evil forest" for being barren.

Chapter Three

Divine Timing

*I*n the Gospel of John, the Bible says that the turning of water into wine by Jesus was the "beginning" of the miraculous signs that authenticated his deity as God in the flesh. As we all know, signs always point to something or someone or someplace, and throughout the scripture we see how all that Christ did and accomplished were all confirmations of all the providential signs that the Old Testament revealed as "types" and "shadows".

Also, when King David was running from his rebellious son Absalom, the Bible says there was "a well without water" over which the woman from Bahurim spread a net to dry her grains as a disguise to hide David and his men (2 Samuel 17:19). We see the parallel in the story of Joseph, a "Type" of Christ thrown into a "well without water" by his envious brothers (Genesis 37:24). In the story of Rehab, the "scarlet rope" tied to her widow (Joshua 2:18-19) was a "sign" pointing to the person of our Lord and Savior Jesus

Christ whose blood is a guarantee for our deliverance as recorded in the New Testament.

My Dad, Mr. Williams was the only surviving child of his mother, therefore, his meeting with the German contractor, the fact that his wife at that point in town went home to have a baby, and the fact that he was never a suspect aiding and abetting my mother's escape were all God's providential plan. His courage to challenge the gods by proposing that my mother be his second wife had a lot to be said about God's invisible hand.

Just get me Pregnant!!

As weeks turned into 6 months, just imagine what it took my dad, to hide a grownup adult in his two-bedroom flat. He refused anyone to visit by giving all kinds of excuses. He kept his window closed and the door locked. He had to look around to ensure no one was watching before opening his door to leave or come into the house.

As God would have it, my stepmother stayed at least two years in the village. At a point, my mother told my dad she cares less about all the gold, fame, wealth, and proms maids and servants she had as a local chief youngest wife since none of that could replace the emptiness or the void of not having a child. She begged my dad to marry her. She estimated that marrying a common man or a 'poor man' would be worth it compare to her present situation of childlessness.

Also, my dad was weary and getting tired of the burden all that was happening had placed on him. The question was for how long he would hold out, as my mother had made it clear that if he insisted that she leaves his place she would jump in front of a moving train which was a common way people commit suicide then.

I want to marry your Sister

On one Friday, right before the end of the day's work, my dad approached Mr. Pius (my uncle), and expressed his weariness and at the same time wiliness to take my mother as his second wife. This was a big turn of events that amounted to the worse situation my uncle would want to be in. How can he oblige to such a request without the proper process and protocol? My uncle told my dad that he would not be responsible for any repercussions of his decision and that he must never mention to anyone that he was aware of this new development.

Marriage in my community is a very important and sacred thing and could be celebrated for weeks as it usually involved a lot of steps and activities before and after the actual marriage itself. The men, women, and the unmarried all play specific roles, and they are presented with gifts usually from the grooms. There would be a lot of food, drinks, and dancing with preparation starting some 18-24 months before the day of marriage. This gives the families enough time to harvest yam tubers and grains like rice which are stored up for the big day depending on the groom's ability to provide such lavish entertainment.

Usually, one or two cows, a male goat, and chickens are selected and nurtured for the day of the marriage. Palm wine (a local extraction from palm trees) is harvested. Also, red oil from the palm tree is prepared, and other items including wrappers and headgears are bought from the local markets to be given out as gifts to family and well-wishers. The dowry, which is the same amount paid by both rich and the poor, is paid to the father of the bride. However, the celebration can be as extravagant and last as many days as the groom can afford to pay the dancers, and musicians as well as provide food for the attendees. In the case of my mum and dad, all of these would not be taking place given the prevailing circumstances in which they found themselves. To make matters worse, my uncle by tradition was forbidden to visit the home of my dad if my mum was there if the needful had not been done by my dad.

I will transfer to Another State

Providentially, my dad's department had a request for an experienced worker who wants to transfer to the northern station which was just built. The transfer came with great promotional pay raise and better housing incentives and so without a doubt, my dad saw this as the sign and an opportunity to marry my mother, and move up north where no one would be able to find out for a long time. It is important to note that at this time migration was not very common but my dad was also at great risk of relocating to a state with a different dialect, and a predominantly Muslim town, Jos in North Central Nigeria. On the day of the journey, my mother was hiding in the cargo area of the train, as she did not want to sit with my dad peradventure someone recognizes her.

The risk was great but she stayed in the cargo section of the train until it made it to another state, a day and a half journey away, before she could join him in the passenger coach and continue the two extra days' journey to Jos, Plateau state.

You are pregnant

Two months after they arrived in the city my mother became sick. At first, they feared this was the effect of a curse on them and they both refused to seek medical attention. However, my dad has had some experience with the early signs of pregnancy and was somewhat relieved when my mother would vomit first thing in the morning. With some trepidation and fear nonetheless, he took her to the Railway Workers Clinic, where a test was conducted which confirmed that my mother was 3 months pregnant. What baffled my mum, was that she menstruated for two months out of the three months she was pregnant, but her fears were allayed when the doctor told her it was not an uncommon manifestation. Explaining further, he told her that she was already pregnant before they embarked on the 3 ½ days journey and that the stress of the journey coupled with the herbs she took for many years may have been responsible for her menstruating during pregnancy.

I am Pregnant

This is the news every mother of a married daughter waits for not too long after marriage because the bride and the groom's mother take turns to visit and help nurse the newborn baby and take care of the woman who has just given birth. So being pregnant after marriage is the dream of every married woman during my mother's era. When in her case for 14 years such news never came to her mother and now she is unable to send word across to her mother that she had delivered, it seemed to cast a shadow over what ordinarily should have been a joyous thing.

What also seemed to compound their problem was that they were in a new state knowing nobody could a young mother nurse her first child. In the case of my stepmother, she had all her children in the village as once she is 6 months pregnant she leaves to stay with my father's mum until she gives birth and stays 2 years thereafter to wean the child. So my dad and mum were thus confronted with taking care of a newborn child without any prior experience for the first time.

My mother's pregnancy progressed very well, and still, nobody from both families knew about it. They never bumped into anyone who might know or recognize them or blow their cover. Amazing indeed, this can only be explained as God's providential hand protecting and shielding them.

It is a boy!!!

Male children are highly valued, cherished, and coveted during my mother's era, and the naming ceremony is very elaborate, with a lot of gifts both for the newborn child. The mother is considered highly blessed and favored, by the gods and the father of the male son walks with extra pride that he now has a son who will succeed him and carry on the family name.

He also has someone who will grow up to assist him in the farm work, hunt for games, and join the male youth to serve in burials, marriages, and other community activities like building fences to protect the community. Those without male sons feel disadvantaged and see themselves as not contributing to the wellbeing of the community as it relates to the youths.

The wives of such men live in perpetual threat and fear believing that they are the cause why their husbands have no male children, oftentimes leading to the men marrying as many wives till they can have a male child. Usually, they will marry younger girls who are sometimes 20 years younger than themselves.

This practice eventually leaves young women to be widowed at an early age when the man dies so much so that the affected women are compelled to do more farm work to survive and raise their young children aside from being sometimes accused of being responsible for her husband's death. In some villages, she will be made to take an oath and this will prevent other men from asking her hand in marriage with the assumption that she might die soon from the curse imposed upon her by the gods.

Female children are considered commodities for sale and gain, and mothers with many girls are considered greedy and selfish because they are the ones who go to the homes of their daughters to help in the nursing of their grandchildren with the attendant material gains, a standing tradition most mothers look forward to while the men stay home. Usually, the man's daughter and her husband can come to visit him or stay with him but not the other way around. It is customarily considered derogatory for a man to stay at his in-law's house.

Custom demands it

As earlier stated, a male child means a lot to the gods, and he is a true pride to the father and community. They are responsible for protection, providing food, farming, hunting, and the general well-being of the community and fighting in a civil war amongst tribal villages if necessary.

Given the above, the naming ceremony of a male child is a special occasion usually done with the killing of goats, while a chicken is offered as a sacrifice to appease the gods, asking for protection, prosperity, and well-being of the male child.

At this point, none of my parents were Christians or believers and held strongly to the belief that there are some laws or customs they cannot tamper with, and feared that if the appropriate sacrifice was not done the male child will die before the age of one. So the clock started ticking from the time my brother was born, with both of my parents virtually ostracized from their villages and families coupled with the fact that my father was an only child and my mother had suffered so much trying to bear a child, this was not a risk they were willing to take… The death of my brother, no way!!

If we die, we die

On January 20, 1959, 24 months after my mum made that daring move, she held her child in her arms. However, both my parents were still in "hiding" as it were so they decided they were going to take the bull by the horn and break every protocol and that they would rather die, and let my brother live. With no precedence to follow except the presence of a divine hand guiding them, they made the first move.

Chapter Four

Taking the bull by the horn

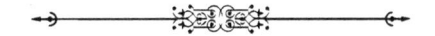

What do we say about the well in Samaria where Jesus met the Samaritan woman? Why was that spot picked for the well during Jacob's days? The only explanation one can conceive is that nothing but the hand of God was planning and orchestrating all things for His glory and praise.

What about the big fish waiting to swallow up Jonah and at the appropriate time and destination vomit Jonah on the shore chosen divinely by God!!

In the case of Joseph, we see that the first place he got to, his brothers were not there, but God divinely positioned a man there to direct Joseph to the location where his brothers were because God in His providence knew and allowed the well/pit to be positioned there as part of the tools God used to bring Joseph to his divine position and place of influence in Egypt.

Talking about the story of Haman and Mordechai, providence positioned Mordechai at the right place, at the right time, to overhear the plot of the two servants against the King. Also, what he did was written in the book of the chronicles of the land and at the appropriate day and time, God providentially allowed the king to be restless because I believe there are other things the king could have chosen to do but he specifically asked for the book of chronicle brought and read to him. In the process, he was reminded that once upon a time his life was in danger and was only spared because Mordechai overheard the plot and foiled it. I believe this was God's plan that the king suddenly asked if the person who foiled the attempted coup was ever rewarded.

Our God, the stage setter

In God's providential plan
- The king sent for Haman the arch-enemy of Mordechai and the Jews;
- The King asked Haman to suggest a reward fitting for someone the King desires to honor
- Haman at this time had already planned how to eliminate the Jews and Mordechai particularly;
- Esther was already the Queen at this time,
- Prayers and fasting were already in place, and we know exactly how the story ended, the people

of God were all spared and the enemy of God destroyed.

God's providential plan allows our enemy to self-destruct period! We see the same scenario played out on the cross as Satan was attempting to have his victory party. Our Lord resurrected crushing Satan's head under His feet hence we have the victorious life in Christ that cannot be duplicated by any.

Even to this day, the Living God is second to none and there is none beside Him. Repeatedly, we read the same phrase in the Old Testament that God will never share His Glory with no one period! It suffices to say that Satan likes to imitate God by setting a look-alike stage hence Apostle Paul advises us not to be ignorant of Satan's devices. History also proved that any other god has no place compared to our Living God who is full of mercy and grace working in mysterious and diverse ways throughout History to date.

So in the case of my parents, God was in full control guiding and leading them even though they were not professed Christians at that time. In God's providential mercy, his hands were revealed in only ways that can be attributed to Him and Him alone. This is especially so because one may reason that what they both did was an abomination and considered adultery in the eyes of man but God judged them differently and blessed them with a baby boy which was considered an acceptance and a blessing by the gods and deity of the land. Even the Bible states that the 'Fear of man is a snare' I guess the saying is right desperate situations call for desperate actions. I can understand my mother's situation but I still cannot get over my Dad taking such a daring action or risk except that he must have had an inner witness of God's Spirit giving him such boldness, though he would always say it is because he is the only child of his mother that drove him to be fearless and bold. I am also sure that hearing the ordeal my mum went through with the local chief, became a strong motivation for his actions.

The full support of my uncle and the cooperation of my mother was more than enough courage for him, he also believed that since the local chief was not honest about his health situation knowing well that my mother being a virgin had no idea that her not being able to get pregnant was not her fault but his.

Fearless Faith versus Faithless Fear

In Judges 4, we are told how a woman took an unusual step and action and how God honored her in return when Israel was going through some dark days. Deborah a Prophetess arose to judge Israel and in her time the enemy was eventually defeated through God providentially using a woman named Jael to defeat the enemy Israel. It is very interesting also to observe that Barak cooperated with Deborah which was unusual except that God's spirit was moving in the heart of Barak as well. Deborah told him that the glory will not be given to him by God but to the hand of a woman.

This importance of this comes to the fore when we understand that at that time women didn't have many rights or say in national affairs. Despite this, Barak affirmative told Deborah that he would only go to battle if Deborah would go with him, showing the providential hand of God at play. In the course of the events, Sisera the enemy fled the battlefield and ran into the tent of Jael, the wife of Heber. Was it then a coincidence that he providentially pitched his tent at the oak of Zaanaim, which is near Kadesh, coincidence or happen-chance? Never!!!

Before any of the characters in Judges 4 even came into this world, God in His providence had set everything in its perfect place and position, just like the Bible says "Grass will wither and flowers will fail, but God's word will never fail"; Israel was God's Chosen nation to bring the good news of our Lord and Savior and because of this God protected and provided all that had to be in place or position for the fulfillment of His divine plan and purpose.

It was all in God's providential plan that even Sisera Chariots of iron were overthrown by the power of God in battle. The Bible also says "From Heaven the stars fought from their courses; they fought against Sisera" which clearly shows that everything created by God will always cooperate with the will of God. Sisera's Chariots of Iron could not withstand the torrents of Kishon, as the ancient river swept them away. To make matters worse, Sisera presumptuously went into the tent of Jael because he thought there was "peace" between Jubin king of Hazor, and the house of Heber, the Husband of Jael. But like Jesus told his disciples, the peace that comes from God is unlike that from the world.

Just imagine the scenario where Sisera asked Jael for water and she wisely gave him milk. The offer of milk in place of water must have given Sisera the impression that Jael was on his side. I would think the water was just fine but given Sisera milk must have given him the wrong confidence that Jeal would align with him to fight against the people of God. She did not only stop there; the Bible said she covered him with a rug, and when he was fast asleep, she took a tent peg and with a hammer drove the peg through his temple. Again we see the hand of providence at work because there was no obvious communication between Deborah, Barak, and Jael, instructing her what to do. Her actions can only be attributed to the Spirit of God working to bring God all the glory and praise just!

God uses Unsanctified Vessels/Situations

Just like in some of the biblical narratives, we see the divine hand of God guiding Rahab to hide the spies on her roof; the same hand also guided her house to be built on the wall creating an easy escape for the spies. Interestingly she was to tie the scarlet rope on her window

Taking the bull by the horn

so that Joshua and others could see it when Jericho was attacked. It is amazing to me that God will use a prostitute, a nobody and a pagan like Rahab to accomplish his plans. Wait a minute do you also realize that this same Rahab a prostitute was the mother of Boaz, an ancestor of Jesus, according to Matthew 1:5.

This story is one of the Bible stories that never ceases to amaze me about God's nature and how he will always be God, he takes no counsel or advice from no one. He decides who to use for what, when, and how all in His perfect control and through His permissive or discretionary will.

Also, we can see that before the spies ever arrived, divine provisions were all in place to ensure God's plan stands and his counsel was established. Rahab's house was erected on the wall; the provision of the flax which she used in covering the spies; the willingness to protect them rather than turn them over to the authorities and the fact that she was aware of how God dealt with the enemies of Israel as they journeyed to the promised land were all God's divine hand at work.

Rahab believed the promise of the spies to protect her and her family and that led her to tie the scarlet rope to the same window from which the spies escaped. We know how the story indeed ended but again and again, we see the hand of God orchestrating circumstances and influencing human hearts to fulfill His purpose.

The story of David and Beersheba which led to the birth of Solomon is another case in point. What was an adulterous union eventually ended up being the lineage of Christ our Lord and Savior! Applying Romans 8:28, we see God using such an unsanctified situation to fulfill his plan for humanity and so one may ask why and how did the spies end up in the house of a prostitute? Can you imagine in our world today, if you were to see a pastor or minister walking into the brothel or the house of a known prostitute and saying the Lord sent him on an errand and that staying in the house of a prostitute was a part of God's plan for them, I am sure none of us will accept such explanation?

What about when Rahab told those who came to arrest the spies that they were not with her and directed them the wrong way whereas she intentionally hid the spies on her roof with flax? Why would the spies even believe her that she was not going to turn them in? Also, why would Rahab believe that the spies will honor their word to her that she and her household will be spared when they come to destroy Jericho? Rahab's house was strategically built on the wall with its windows also placed to enable the spies to leave without being noticed, does that not show how God's providential hand and purpose were being played out here.

In the account of Joseph and the false accusation of Potiphar's wife, so he could end up in prison, we see this seeming "setback" eventually leading to his becoming second in command in Egypt. I have sometimes wondered what the fate of Potiphar and his wife would be after

Taking the bull by the horn

Joseph whom they once ruled over and threw in prison suddenly become their ruler overnight. There is a lesson to be learned here so that we may be careful how we treat people we meet because we can never know what God has in stock for them. One prayer I have learned to pray is that God should help me not to fight those whom he has sent to be my divine helpers.

In prison, Joseph found favor with the keeper of the prison so much so he made Joseph be in charge of other prisoners. This may seem ordinary but when we remember that it was what led him to connect with Pharaoh's Baker and Butler two men who had dreams that he interpreted we recognize once again God's providential grace enabling Joseph was able to interpret the dreams they had. This was instrumental to the Butler recommending Joseph to Pharaoh when all his magicians could not interpret that particular dream even though they have been interpreting dreams for Pharaoh before. I believe what happened is that God made it impossible for the magicians to interpret that dream because it was Joseph's hour of glory.

Furthermore, the fact that the Butler forgot about Joseph for two good years and the slim chance of recalling the promise he made to Joseph are things to consider. In my opinion, the sincere request that Joseph asked of him not to forget about him but mention him to Pharaoh, was so he could be released and reunited with his family in Canaan. But God had a bigger and better plan for him and God's plan for Joseph's release was way bigger than Joseph could ever imagine or wrap his mind around. Sometimes that is exactly what happens in our individual lives when God's providential plans begin to unfold with difficulties and inconveniences all around us so that we cannot imagine how a good God allows us to pass through difficulties and pains and sometimes question God's supreme power to control things, event, and humans.

The First Telegram

My mother's brother was still a prime suspect with no means of communication other than through telegram or letters. There was no way to let their families know about their welfare, except by two handwriting notes my dad gave the Train conductor to hand deliver to my uncle in Lagos. At the time that was the fastest and safest way to get mail as letters through post often takes weeks to arrive. When my uncle received the notes it gave him some level of peace that my mother was doing well and he was willing to continue taking the risk on their behalf as long as it gives my mother the lifelong joy of having her child.

My Grandparents – The Aigbes

After 6 months of not knowing about my mother's whereabouts, my uncle received a message from his parents that they had contacted an oracle that confirmed my mother was alive and well. The oracle also told them my mother was with a man, and that some good news was coming their way.

With this information, my mother's brother made the bold move to go see his parents face to face. He also made sure he got home when it was dark for fear someone might see him and eardrop on his conversation with his parents. Since his parents had no foreknowledge he would be visiting, he sneaked into his father's compound and tapped on his mother's door who opened the door to see her son unexpectedly appear before her. After he had a short talk with her, she proceeded to call his father and the three had a heart-to-heart talk during which time he gave details about all that transpired to them and the good news of the birth of my brother. When the good news of the arrival of a grandchild was broken to them their joy knew no bounds but they still had to tread softly as my mother was still considered a fugitive at that time. That same night my uncle slept for only two hours after which his father took him on his bicycle to the driver's house secretly.

Breaking the News

With great fear and concern about how the local chief would react to this news about my mother, they decided that it was best to send a telegram directly to him asking him to release her from the marriage vow she took with him. What this meant was that some traditional rites would have to be performed and my grandparents, the Aigbes were willing to pay whatever it will take to resolve the impasse. The traditional rites would involve animal sacrifice and the return of the dowry, which must come directly from the man who intends to marry her. In our tradition, the dowry is an exact amount that cannot be negotiated.

Second Telegram

My mother sent a telegram to the local chief explaining herself and that she was sorry and asked him to forgive her while ending the note that she had given birth to a baby boy. She further asked for his blessings. On receiving the telegram, the local chief summoned my grandparents, the Aigbes to a meeting. When they arrived they both pretended as if this was the first time they are hearing about what happened otherwise they will be charged with breach of the marriage contract. With mixed emotions of fear and relief, they begged the local chief to release my mother from the marriage and all curses associated with her actions. After much deliberations, a date was set for the traditional annulment of the marriage between my mother and the local chief, although he was still very angry and even demanded that my grandparents give him another of their daughters in exchange; a tradition which was accepted then. Unfortunately for the local chief, as faith would have it, my grandparent's youngest daughter was already married with two children, and their only child at home was a male child. Eventually, the local chief decided to let go and accepted the return of the dowry with all the necessary animal sacrifices that needed to be done to appease the gods.

Double Celebration

Exactly 18 months after my mother gave birth to a son, all the marital annulment rites and sacrifices were made with the full dowry returned to the local chief by my dad. As the marriage rites and tradition between my parents were being performed right after the annulment of that with the local chief in my grandparents' house, it was a day of sadness in the family of the local chief and joy in my paternal and maternal grandparents' house.

My parents dare not attend any of the ceremonies, but a representative was sent from my father to the local chief, and on that fateful day my mother was officially freed from the marriage vow she made with the local chief and was now officially his wife. We can see the unseen hand of God providentially evident as the story unfolds. Now my grandparents were free to celebrate the birth of their grandson, my brother, without any fear of retribution from the local chief or the gods.

In Africa, the celebration of the arrival of a grandchild is very important particularly from a grandparent's standpoint, because having a grandchild moved them to a different level within the community. It is also important because when they die the type and extent of the burial ceremony are determined by whether they have grandchildren or not. Those who die without grandchildren are buried hurriedly within 24 hours of their death within the community burial ground whereas those who have grandchildren are buried on family land chosen by their surviving children.

With the arrival of a child, a white chalk-like powder is used to mark the joyous news as grandparents move from house to house sharing the grounded white chalk with every woman within the community. This ritual is continued up till the very next market day which is usually held weekly or bi-weekly. The same process is repeated at the market where the grandparents take the same white chalk-like powder and share with other women in the local market the news of the arrival of a grandchild.

They changed their mind

My maternal grandmother took the celebration to a different level, she gathered some women and organized a dance group that danced around the market and she used a megaphone to announce that her daughter who was labeled barren has given birth to a son and doing so in a local market place helped to spread the news far and wide in a bid to vindicate her family and erase the scandal that her daughter ran away from her husband the local chief, something unheard of and considered an abomination. Most of them expected the death of her daughter so they could easily conclude that the gods punished her for her action.

Being also traditional people my grandparents to some extent also believed my mum could be under a curse and were expecting the news of her passing away. Their fear was based particularly on the fact that my mum gave birth before the customary ceremony was done to return the local chief's dowry and such restitution was not done in that order. The dowry should have been returned and accepted before the new husband could touch or have anything to do with her but we see the providential hand of God overruling all their superstitious beliefs and protecting my mother and my father.

It is a general belief that the gods will kill any woman who sleeps with another man while she is legally married and more so if she was married to a local chief whom they believe the gods would have greater protection for.

If my mother had passed away or died at childbirth it would have been concluded that the gods had punished her and sadly a lot of women who died during childbirth in that era were all attributed to being victims of retribution by the gods assuming the woman must have committed adultery against her husband somewhere somehow. So you can just imagine what the state of mind my grandparents were when they heard that my mother gave birth to a son and that she and the son and the father to the son are all alive and well!

Abraham went not knowing but knew He who knows

This whole story was narrated to me by my parents and my grandparents from both sides with my uncles and aunts confirming it as true. I also visited my maternal village and saw the local chief's two-story stone building standing with distinct characteristics and quite different from all the other surrounding buildings. I must confess that a nostalgic feeling ran through my vein that left me with a lot of questions than answers. I thought of all that I could have had, should have had; all the "buts" and "ifs". Coming to faith at the age of 18 after all the events and circumstances in my personal life it took a real quest on my side to know God on a very personal and to acknowledge that my real-life experiences are not unique. I came to realize what our father of faith, Abraham must have passed through in his walk with God. I reckoned that even though my mother was not a confessed Christian neither was my dad at that time the scripture "He has set eternity in their hearts" explains how God through his providential will orchestrated all that eventually worked "together for good" for my parents.

Just as Romans 1:20 says "for the invisible things of him from the creation of the world are seen, being understood by the things that are made, even His eternal power and Godhead, so that they are without excuse" is self-evident in my parents' story. They like Abraham were made to leave their "country", family, and kindred, and go to a place where they didn't know. All the while the hand of God leading and sustaining them. And in Hebrew 11 the bible states categorically that Abraham went not knowing where he was going. In hindsight, we can see that the scripture in Romans 1:17 which says "Abraham being declared righteous lived by faith" came alive in Abraham when he obeyed!

When we examine the life of Moses, the scriptures confirm that he obeyed God even though he was brought up in Pharaoh's palace without formal knowledge of the God of the people of Israel. You will also agree with me that from the time Joseph's brothers decided to sell him into slavery God had already predestined that Moses will be born in Egypt and that the Pharaoh who knew Joseph would die giving rise to another Pharaoh who will sort to kill Moses because Moses killed an Egyptian. This same Pharaoh will begin to feel threatened by the population rise of the children of Israel and would seek a "Jewish solution". All these and much more are the unseen and providential hands of the almighty God in the event of mankind bringing about His divine purpose in our individual lives.

God, I had questions that no one could answer, and I began to find the answers in the scriptures. It was truly humbling to read about the hand of God working in the lives of different Bible characters like Abraham and Isaac, showing me the difference between the perfect will and the permissive will of God which helped me to clear my doubts.

God showed his perfect will in the life of Abraham who was instructed to sacrifice his son, after which He provided a ram caught in the thicket on the mountain for a replacement. We also see this dichotomy in the story of God choosing Esau over Jacob, Ephraim over Manasseh, Moses over all the children born in his time, Samuel over every other child born to Elkanah and over the children of Eli, God choosing to anoint David (passing over the older sons of Jesse) even when Saul was still king, and God choosing Mary over all the women in Israel to bear Jesus.

Through my constant search for knowledge and understanding of God, the word 'providence' began to surface in my mind every time I tried to rationalize what my mother and father went through bringing my siblings and me, to the world. I wish I could tell you that all through the process of having my siblings and me, my mum's life was smooth and rosy but it was the complete opposite. She went through horrible times, experiencing hunger and lack, fear and uncertainty.

Recall that my mother was initially married to a local chief in her village but she had to leave the marriage to find happiness and fulfillment. The difficulties she went through as a result of this decision were great. But even in times of emotional torture, hardship and fear, she would always say to me that God gave her everything she desired and that was enough for her. I can recall days when my mum would have to cook bones for us to eat in place of meat. She would always express her thanks to God who gave her children to feed with the bones. I remember wondering for years if she had made the right decision by leaving the Chief and if our lives would have been better otherwise, but it wasn't until I got into the healthcare profession that I began to understand her decision. She left the local chief because she realized that though he had children from his senior wives, he couldn't have any through her.

For a long time, I didn't believe that she had made a wise decision. Who leaves affluence in marriage to leave in hardship? Over the past 9 years, through my relationship with God, I have come to understand and appreciate her. I thank God that she decided to leave the 'good life' that marrying a local chief would have afforded her. I might have never found Christ without what she went through.

At the time of writing this book, all the Chief's children who were born before I was born are dead, his stone house empty, his other property in bad shape and his name only draws old stories of intimidation, fear, idolatry, and superstition. As more people in the village turn to Christianity, fully grasping the sacrifice of Christ on the cross, the animal sacrifices carried out in his house have become obsolete. The eating of sacrificed meat, which was a daily occurrence in his house, is now a relic of the past.

Chapter Five

My Dysfunctional Family

After my father's wife returned from nursing her 6th child, my father and mother had to live in different cities. My father lived with my stepmother in Jos, and my mother and her children lived in Kafanchan (both cities are in Plateau State in the northern part of Nigeria). This was because my stepmother would harass my mother constantly with a tirade of insults and my mother would just look with joyful eyes, sometimes even bursting into songs of praise in the heat of the moment. I could never understand why she never fought back because my mother looked like the stronger of both women.

As a child, I would always promise my mother that I would defend her when I got older and I got the chance to do so when I was 9 years old. It was the holidays and we had not seen my father for over a year. My mother decided to take us (my two brothers and I) on the early morning train over to Jos to see him. Unfortunately, he had already left for work when we got there but we met my stepmother. First, she didn't let us into the house, then she proceeded to pour dirty water on my mother. At this point I had had enough, I took a whip and flogged her. My older brother and I unleashed our anger on her while my mother stood by and watched telling her that her day of reckoning was at hand. My stepmom's children were not home so we had our way and then left the house, immediately heading back home to Kafanchan. That was the last time my stepmother and my mother ever fought. My father was furious when he got back, he came to our house to tell us how unhappy he was with our outburst. We never visited him in Jos again, instead, he would come and spend a night with us in Kafanchan and then leave the next morning on the first train to Jos.

Message from my Paternal Grandmother

When my mother was six weeks pregnant with me, my father got a message via the telegram from his mother saying that I was a reincarnation of her late sister and that my name would be "Omoyemen" meaning "Child is precious". At this point, my mother didn't even know that she was pregnant with me. My mom spoke to a friend who advised her to go for prayers at a local church. My mum was not a believer at that time but she had decided to stop serving idols and had left all that behind her so she was scared that some spirits were actually after her and her baby.

Thank God she took the advice of her friend and started her journey with the Lord. From that day until the day she died, she was actively involved in the Apostolic Church in Kafanchan. My father also became a Christian sometime later. This also became a thing of shame for me because other children had both their parents take them to church or school but I could never have my father in those places for me. One time, a brother from the church had to stand in as my brother's guardian to take him to school. Seeing my father only two times a year was hard enough, knowing that he would only spend nights and leave early in the morning was even worse. I always wished that my siblings would be awake when my dad came to visit or that he would just stay long enough to go to church with us so we could hold hands in public but it never happened.

Sometimes, I would intentionally fall in public so that a man that I considered a father figure would pick me up and rock me. I did this so much that my mother took me to see a doctor, thinking there was something wrong with my legs. Thank God, she never gave me medication to that effect but just focused on praying for strength in my legs.

One of my prayers somewhat came to pass when my father asked that one of his children go and stay with his mother who was living by herself because my step-sister that was living with her getting married. I immediately jumped at this opportunity, telling him that I would love to go and stay with her. My mother was absolutely surprised and livid. She insisted that I would not leave and this led to an argument between us. Here I was, asking to go and be with a grandmother that I had never met and who lived so far away that it would take 5 days by train to get there (She lived in the then Bendel State, now Edo state in the southern part of Nigeria).

If she must go

My mother insisted that if I must go, my younger brother who was 9 years old at the time and the only surviving twin that my mum had, must go with me. Both my parents agreed and then my mother took my 9-year-old brother, my 7-year-old brother, and me on the arduous 5-day journey to the village my grandmother lived. It was a bitter-sweet experience for her because she was also from the village and this was a chance to see her family after a long time but it was also the first time she would be returning to the village after running away from her first husband, the local chief Ogedegbe.

For me, this was a great experience because I got to be miles away from my father so I could rationalize his absence and it also confirmed that my siblings and I were his children. My stepmother made it a point to always let us know that we were not my father's children even up to the point of getting her children to tell us not to call 'their father' daddy anymore. Taking us to his mother showed me acceptance and this made me happy. It's pretty normal to call people who are not your parents 'Daddy' and 'Mummy.' Today, by the grace of God I have a lot of spiritual sons and daughters who call me Mom and Grandma and I have no problems with it. But at that point in my life, it brought me so much hurt whenever my stepmother told me that my siblings and I were not my father's even though we were. I carried this shame and pain for years into my adulthood.

Living-it-out with my Paternal Grandmother

There ancient saying that goes, we may choose our actions but we do not have control over the consequences. Back in the Northern part of the country, my parents stayed in separate cities when I was younger. This was something I hated so much that I decided to carry out a scheme of faking falls whenever an adult male was close by just to get the 'fatherly' attention I desired. Unbeknownst to me, this created great concern for my mom. My dad was also worried because it never happened when he was with me. Whenever I was around him, I did not need fake anything.

I recall never leaving his sight at night and when he would leave by taking the last train back to Jos, I would stay up all through pretending to be asleep and when he would quietly bid us goodbye at midnight, I recall getting up to hug him while my brothers were fast asleep. He would then tiptoe behind them, then walk out to the car waiting to take him to the train station.

Now with my paternal grandmother, my mother expressed the fear of my constant falls to her and that led my grandmother on a journey to find answers since my mother had told her that the doctors could not find the cause. She resorted to seeking alternative remedies and she was told by one herbalist that the gods of the waters were responsible for my constant falls and that I was a 'key' holder to the water spirits. The herbalist specifically instructed my grandma not to allow me to go close to any river. This was so exaggerated and coupled with the fact that I had a near-drowning experience when I was about 7yrs old, it created a serious water phobia in me. My grandma built an earthen altar in her house for me dedicated to the water spirits. This led to serious exposure to idol worshiping and when the news got to my mother, she was very unhappy and which created a prolonged quarrel between her and my grandmother.

Every attempt to remove me from my grandma's care was unfruitful. I never wanted to leave because I felt more secure knowing that I was living in my father's house which some extent helped ease my pain. I never had to face the ridicule of other kids mocking me to leave their father alone, instead, the children in the village held me in high esteem, constantly asking me what the city looks like because most of them had never traveled out of the village. I also got away with a lot of mistakes that the other kids got in trouble for.

For example, I would climb trees that I had no idea who they belonged to and the other kids would quickly report to my parents knowing that I wouldn't be punished but they would. Besides, I was academically more advanced than most of them. I could read and speak good English that was way beyond their standards because most of them had a late start at school due to financial constraints. This placed me at a great advantage socially. I was also a beautiful child by all standards. I took after my dad's light complexion and build. The fact that I looked just like my dad, who was a very handsome man, made me my grandma's favorite grandchild and she vowed to protect me with all the unbiblical methods she could muster since she attributed my academic prowess, beauty, and social likeness to the god of the waters.

I was also a favorite of my paternal grandfather. My grandmother always showed her love for me by making sure my school fees were paid on time.

Chapter Six

Experience versus Head Knowledge

Simply knowing the truth that makes us free is not sufficient. We must have experiential knowledge also; that is the transition from head knowledge to heart knowledge. There are two types of belief: believing with the mind and believing with the heart. There is a great difference between these two kinds of beliefs. I once heard it said that 'the greatest distance in the world is the eighteen inches between our head and our mind.'

It is one thing to know something in your mind and an entirely different thing to believe it in your heart. This is exemplified in the miraculous work of forgiveness that we witness so often. We see it at work when a person believes that he has done something too terrible to be forgiven, only to then hear the truth that God loves him despite what he has done and that God is willing to forgive him if he accepts God's gift forgiveness. Oh, what a level of peace one experiences when that marvelous transformation occurs, once the transition from head-knowledge to heart-knowledge takes place and we realize that we are forgiven dearly and perfectly loved.

The following are steps we can apply to free us from shame:

Confession: This helps to eliminate all roots of guilt. Confess every suspected guilt which includes all sins which one is aware of or recalls. Confess your faults to another person, that person may be a prayer partner or a minister of the word. James 5:16a, 'Confess your faults one to another, and pray one for another, that you may be healed.' However, I must caution that you must make sure such a person is a trusted and mature believer who will not take advantage of your confession to slander you.

Discernment: Pray for self-discernment and to be reminded of any person who may have wronged you. Pray for the Holy Spirit to search your hearts. Jeremiah 17: 9, 'the heart is deceitful above all things, desperately wicked: who can know it?' It is appropriate to pray that God should search us and try to reveal to us all our shortcomings, so that we may repent of them and become righteous before Him.

Forgiveness: We must forgive every person who may have wronged or hurt us. Non-forgiveness is another often overlooked area of sin. It gives the tormentors a legal right to attack us. Matthew 18:34-35 says, 'and His Lord was angered and delivered him to the tormentors, till he should pay all that was due unto Him, so likewise shall my heavenly Father do also unto you if you from your hearts forgive not everyone his brother their trespasses.' Luke 6:28 says, 'Bless them that curse you, and pray for them which despitefully use you.' So, forgive them and ask God to forgive them as well.

Repentance: Repent not only of every known sin but also every area of known or unknown disobedience to the Lord, His word, His will, or direction for our life (all sins of commission and omission). Revelation 3:19, 'as many as I love, I rebuke and chasten, be zealous therefore, and repent.'

Love: Love everyone, as much as you are capable, especially those of the household of God (Believers). Ephesian 5:1-2a says,

> "Be ye, therefore followers of God, as dear children; and walk in love, as Christ also hath loved us, and hath given Himself for us an offering and a sacrifice to God for a sweet-smelling savor."

John 13:35 says,

> "By this, shall all men know that ye are my disciples if ye have love one to another"

John 15:12 also says

> "This is my commandment, that ye love one another as I have loved you."

Deliverance: A person must be delivered from all related spirits. We must cast out every evil spirit whose presence we suspect, especially the spirit of timidity. Pray for boldness Acts 4:29-31 says,

> "And now lord behold their threatening: and grant unto thy servants that with all boldness they may speak thy word. By stretching forth thine hand to heal and that signs and wonders may be done by the name of thy holy child Jesus. And when they had prayed, the place was shaken where they were assembled, and they were all filled with the Holy Spirit, and they spoke the word of God with Boldness."

A careful analysis of the ministry of Jesus showed that he always conducted deliverance by casting out demons from people. Jesus was the exemplary deliverance minister!

The evidence that we have been delivered from shame is our ability to bear reproach for the sake of the Gospel. 1 Peter 4:16,

> "Yet if any man suffers as a Christian, let him not be ashamed; but let him glorify God on this behalf."

Acts 5: 41 says,

> "And they departed from the presence of the council, rejoicing that they were counted worthy to suffer shame (disgrace) for His name."

There are times in our lives when being ashamed may not be a bad thing. In fact, in the text above, the apostles were imprisoned and beaten because they had healed a multitude of sick people, and those who were possessed by unclean spirits. As a result, the chastised apostles rejoiced because they had suffered disgrace for the sake of the gospel. We, therefore, discover an important truth. When we have on the armor of righteousness and are shamed or disgraced, it does not bother us all; on the contrary, we are blessed.

Glory on the other hand is the opposite of shame. Just as Jesus traded shame for eternal glory, so God has promised that we will one day share in His magnificent Glory. And the Lord has made it abundantly clear that His will is for us to be shame-free here on earth.

My paternal grandfather also decided to pamper me, and he would always call me to give me a treat whenever he comes back from the farm, like a piece of well ripe mango, roasted crickets, or roasted yam, every day I looked forward to his coming back from the farm, I finally got the signal that he was not doing so to other children, on his way back from the farm he would stop by my grandma's chamber and ask me to bring him water to drink after a couple of times I would look out for his coming which was a clockwork, he arrives almost the same time every day, have the cup of water ready and work with him to his chamber he would look at me with an impressive broad smile and say you will go far.

When I took part in the Common Entrance Examination for what was called the secondary school (which is the equivalent of middle and high school here) I was the only student from my grandma's village that passed in my entire class of over 40 students. This made me even more popular amongst my peers, I had four possible schools to choose from but my mother insisted that I should go to one of the schools outside my city whereas both my grandparents insisted that I should attend the school in my city so they can keep an eye on me.

My mother being hundreds of miles away, could not enforce her wish which was to remove me from my grandma's grip and idol worship. Instead, my academic success made my grandma intensify her search for protection from the gods and this meant I had to wear some white gowns she made for me and attend the sacred day of worship of the water spirit which falls every Sunday afternoon. My grandpa was the local priest and he had a part of his compound painted with white chalk and an altar made where he would pour some palm wine after some prayers/incantations with words that I didn't understand. During the ceremony, my grandma and other women would sit, sing, and dance, and to my surprise, I was the only child among them. I was to learn that though I was the only child physically present in the spirit realm they claimed I was a priestess and superior in their spiritual hierarchy.

Throughout my stay with my grandparents, I never went to church from age 10 to 12, but I believed looking back that my mother never stopped praying, and as I will elaborate on later, my mother believed in prayers and did a lot of it for me.

Retired moving back home for Good

It was my 2nd year in high school and without any prior knowledge, both my parents and stepmother arrived with a big truck full of belonging. I was truly confused as I could not articulate what was going on but there was a lot of jubilation, particularly from my paternal grandmother who praised the gods for not allowing their son to die "abroad". I later found out that it was common for most families never to get the opportunity to bury their loved ones who left the village for greener pastures and end up dying abroad. This was so because transporting a dead body was not practical or feasible then and so it was seen and held as a curse if the dead did not get to be buried in the tribal burial ground with all the traditional rituals performed. They believed that such an individual's spirit will roam forever.

Open Vindication

Words fail me to express the kind of joy I saw in my mother when she came back to the village alive. I saw the side of her I never knew existed, fearless, bold, and daring! My dad had his living section in my grandfather's chambers, which had 3 rooms, one for my mother and one for my stepmother while my dad's slept in the third room.

My maternal uncle was financially stable being self-employed and in the cocoa business. With him and other of my mother's siblings, came a tremendous outpouring of support both financially and materially. My uncle furnished my mother's room which made my stepmother demand that my father furnish her room as well. My father did not respond to her demand and every day my stepmother would start the day with cursing but not for long, as this gave me another opportunity that I have always wanted to her disbelief I repeated what I did at the age of 9 in Jos, after which I ran and stayed with my maternal grandmother until my dad's anger subsided. This was the last open confrontation my mother ever had with my stepmother!

I was my paternal grandfather's favorite and he took special likeness in me, especially because of my academic achievement. My mother was a seamstress but moving back home meant her business suffered a lack of enough patronage so she decided to own a mini cold drink and snack store along the express highway meaning she would be gone almost all day from the house. Although this idea was supported by my father, it did not go well with my paternal grandmother specifically because she saw it as a sleek way of losing her grip on me.

On the other hand, my mother was happy because I stopped attending all the weekly worship of water gods. This also did not go well with my maternal grandmother, as my mother insisted I go into the boarding school which further separated me from idol worship coupled with the fact the arrival of my mother meant that she always took us to church. For her attending church was mandatory.

Chapter Seven

My School Years–St. Dominic

*N*ow, being in a Catholic school was somewhat a true getaway as I was free from being forced to participate in fetish activities. At the boarding school, however, attending Mass and Sunday service was mandatory. Most of my teachers were Nuns, which again elicited another phase of shame and guilt. Most of my fellow students already have some kind of church-going experience and were familiar with the catholic doctrines and rituals and it was unnerving to discover that among my schoolmates I was the only one who had an idol altar dedicated to me at my age.

Whenever I related the story, it sounded very strange to them. Again, I began to feel different suddenly all the shame and guilt re-surfaced. I continue to ask why everything seems different in my life, I thought I had escaped that emotional battle now that my dad had retired to move back home with my mother even though seeing my dad was still scarce because he picked up a security job at the local government council which meant he was gone most of the day. I decided to intentionally distance myself from my schoolmate by constant reading and studying which ended up being of benefit to me academically. They all have stories about the relationship with their dad and I do not have any; so I continued to live a recluse lifestyle even into my middle school years.

Senior years at St. Dominic

At Senior College, we were separated into two career groups for the last two years, and this was based strictly on how well one performed in the science or art examination. To my greatest surprise, I was the only female student who scored enough to be selected for the science group. This turned out to be a blessing in disguise.

I found out that boys do not seem to ask too many questions like the female students and most of them do not have interesting stories about their dad, all they talk about is studies and careers! This was a perfect place to be, so I was able to hide my shame and guilt.

Being the only female science student in my class has its benefit, I was well known among the students, and lecturers, also I was completely exempted from all the Saturday chores and cleaning, since the physics and chemistry labs held on Saturdays. I stood out, always among boys for group studies and assignments, while they

My School Years–St. Dominic

competed to be my best friend and helper, this placed a great deal of pressure on me to succeed and excel. I still carried a great deal of shame and guilt with me particularly when I recall the resentments from my step-siblings, it was manageable with my two step-brothers, BUT it was a nightmare with my 3 step sisters.

Oh, how I wished to be accepted by them, particularly when I see a relationship between an older sister and a younger one. The hand-down of clothes and shoes they always displayed once we came back from holidays gives me plenty of pain knowing how much I could get from the three of my female stepsisters. Someone would always ask if I am the oldest daughter, or if I have an older sister(s) and I wished I could yes since saying no fits the obvious narrative. But then again saying yes exposes all my pains the more, having to explain why I and my maternal siblings were so rejected and disliked by my step-mother and all five of my step-siblings for reasons that I and my siblings did not create.

The jealousy and envy were further aggravated when I became the first female among my father's children to go to college since my step sisters all got married after basic elementary education. For reasons I never understood, in a bid to counter their hatred, my mother would always tell me that I must go to college even if it meant her borrowing money. Since education was not free at that time, I believe parents have to choose which of their children they would invest in financially. This became a blessing in disguise as I used studying as an escape from my pains.

Almost all the lecturers and a good number of the male students took a likeness to me but there were a good number of fellow female students who just could not stand my presence. They called me proud and arrogant meanwhile I felt less than that on the inside and was carrying a load of shame and guilt in my heart. Providence had it that the physics, biology, and chemistry labs were open on Saturdays, which is also one of the visiting days for parents. Literally "hiding" there shielded me from the famous question of "where is your dad"? I discovered that some students faked a fainting attack to avoid being embarrassed but such a prank would work against me and make them hospitalize me which meant missing out on lectures.

Besides I also found out that most people who faint and fall had epilepsy which made people run from them so that trick was not contemplated by me. Saturday and Sundays were parental visiting days while it was mandatory to attend mass on Sundays. Visiting Parents also use this visiting time to replenish their children's provisions, so I decided after lectures on Saturdays and Church service on Sundays, I would always go to one of the classrooms to study.

I also discovered that only a few of the boys get visited so they too used that time to study particularly the science students so I fitted just right in, as most of them concluded that I have asked my parents not to "disturb me with visit" since I was a science student. Two of the lecturers knew my mother from her retail store business and will always bring me words from her, which also made me feel somehow special when they extend such greetings to me from my mother to the hearing of other students.

My godmother

In St Dominic, we had 4 wings in the female dormitory, and each wing has a prefect and then a senior prefect. Right from my first year, I noticed that there was a practice called "goddaughter and godmother relation" and it involved the goddaughter writing one of the older female students to be her godmother. The boys did the same, but I was not too keen on selecting a godmother as this will expose me to talk about my family which I was not ready to do. So I watched as others engaged in finding a godmother or godfather.

This relationship is very involving as it meant sharing provisions, the goddaughter washings the godmother's clothing, and serving her. I also observed that it is always the goddaughter that initiates the relationship but in my case, I was hardly in the dormitory and only came back late just to shower and sleep. In the cafeteria, I would usually see the goddaughter collecting food for their godmothers and taking it to the dormitory. Most godmothers had a small stove they use to cook but eating in the cafeteria was a must for me come rain or shine.

On a fateful day when I got to the dormitory, I was told that the senior dormitory prefect wants to see me. I was afraid, thinking I had just done something wrong that had been reported to her. To my greatest surprise, she handed me a note with a smile on her face and insisted I read it in her presence. While four other students (her goddaughters) stood by, with shaking hands, I opened and read that she is asking me to be her goddaughter. Only a big fool would refuse such an offer, she added that she understood that the reason why I had not chosen a godmother was that I could not meet the demand of such a relationship and I need not worry.

I also found out that I was the youngest among her four goddaughters, and that her junior brother was in my set though not in the science class. She said her brother spoke highly of me. At that time she was in her final year while I had 18 more months to go. For the first time I felt good on the inside that I was not only going to have her as my godmother but an older sister I so longed for. She was very petite, which made me fit in her used clothes. The other goddaughters chose her because of her position not necessarily because they needed any material benefit from her; instead, they would bring all their provisions and store them in her care for all to share. I was very careful not to get indulged since I was not contributing much, I would excuse myself by saying those provisions make me sleepy and I will not be able to stay awake to study. This was a good excuse since none of the other goddaughters were in the science class.

I could not wait to tell my mother of this wonderful news. While on spring break she asked if I could come to spend the holiday with her; so just before our last day of school, she went to see my mother introduce herself as my godmother, and promised she will take good care of me. She told my mother not to worry about provisions for me and also asked for permission for me to spend the holiday with her. Such an offer was too good to reject, as my mother saw this as filling a void in my life since I had no older female to look up to. She was very protective of me, and she made all the male senior students know that they could try to propose any boyfriend/girlfriend relationship with me. I had no idea why she would go to that length to protect me except for the fact that she knew I was very naïve and innocent. I concluded she just was helping me stay on course because we had some girls that had to drop out of school after they got pregnant.

In school, I was focused on my studies because I did not want to disappoint my mother being the first female among my dad's children to attain such a level of education. It was an honor I did not want to play with, so armed with this and the fact that my mother warned me that committing an abortion could take my life, I never allowed myself to lose track of my dream. I remembered what she went through before having children so the thought of having an abortion scared me. Looking back under my godmother's watchful eyes and the threat from my mother I was able to survive all the pressure from men and boys wanting to have an intimate relationship with me. Even when my godmother graduated, I was not enticed, having just one year to graduate.

Send off Party

Now classes were over and we were studying for our SCHOOL LEAVING CERTIFICATE, a test that enables one to gain admission into the universities. We had 90 days to the examination, when my godmother visited me and brought me some provisions, and told me to come to visit her on the last Friday of school to collect the clothes and shoes she bought for me to attend the school's send-off party. At this time the seniors were free to leave the dormitory without permission, as long they arrive before the 9 pm curfew. However, most will arrive later than 9 pm and scale the fence, usually with one of their goddaughter or godson watching and listening for a knock on the window to let them in. Also, all the seniors were housed in one of the units, and the nightly headcount at 8 pm did not include them they had barely three months to graduation.

As planned I visited my godmother at her house and she handed me a bag which I believed contained the clothes she promised and with her was a young man whom she introduced as her immediate senior brother based in a city, called Lagos. He was a staff of the Federal Ministry of Finance, in the Visa and International Students Department. She was quick to tell me that he was the one who bought the clothes and shoes from Lagos. I took a peek inside the bag and they were brand new clothes and a pair of new shoes. I immediately thanked him and my godmother. I did not make anything out of it till he left and came back with some drinks and cookies. I could tell from the look of the drinks that I had never tasted this type before, he insisted that this was a celebration of my achievement and that he has heard so much about me. I took a sip and being the very first time I tested a drink with alcohol, I became tipsy and somewhat drowsy.

It was also getting dark and so she suggested that I spent the night at her house. I have slept in her family house before so passing the night was not an issue, until I found out that I was not going to share her bed with her but with her brother. I was 17 at this time and had never been in a room with a male with the door closed. Both parents were at home and his mom came into the room and greeted me so affectionately that I was given more to drink and got tipsy.

In the room, he encouraged me to lay down which I gladly did and that was all I could recollect. When I woke up early the next morning I found out that he had slept on the same bed with me and I felt different and knew he must have had an intimate relationship with me. Right there he told me he was madly in love with me and would want me to join him in Lagos to pursue the possibility of traveling abroad for further studies with him. He also invited me to travel to the nearest city with him to visit a former classmate; he spoke a lot that morning but all I kept thinking about was what must have happened to me.

When I went to take a shower I noticed my undergarments were soiled with blood, and I know this was not my menstruation, since I just completed a circle two weeks earlier. Returning from the shower, my godmother came in and brought me some underwear, and clothes to wear since I had brought none. That was how I lost my virginity to my godmother's brother. All through the day, he kept him saying how much he loves me and wants to be with me.

After the morning breakfast which his mom prepared and serve to both of us in his room, the whole house became quiet. His mom had gone to the local market with my godmother, his father also had gone to work being an elementary school teacher; his junior brother who had come home from school also left leaving just the two of us. He had a field day and he had an intimate relationship with me, without much resistance from me. After that we left to visit his friend and there he introduced me as his fiancée, I simply just played along. On returning, he stopped and bought me more provisions, went with me to my school where we spent the whole evening together, within the school compound and he left after giving me some money.

I had two months to my final examination so because I was focused on my studies I did not realize that I had missed my menstrual cycle. After the exam finished, my godmother, invited me again to come over, this time she had planned with her brother not to let me out of their sights. At this point, my mother never knew that my godmother's brother had slept with me.

After about two months, I was now conscious that I had not seen my menstruation and my godmother told me she believed I was pregnant from the nights I slept with her brother assuring me that she will not tell anyone. She told me she will help me abort the child so that our secrets will be hidden. So she gave me some pills to take, unbeknown to me they were vitamins. A few days later her brother came from the city and invited me to join him to pursue the visa process. I did not mention anything about the pregnancy to anyone since my godmother told me not to tell anyone. That very weekend I visited my mother accompanied by my godmother to share with her the prospect of traveling abroad for further studies. My godmother assured my mother that she need not worry that her brother works in the Federal Ministry of Finance and will be able to finance my studies. My beloved mother thanked her so much and prayed for God's blessings upon her.

In the City

Here I was just 17 plus in a big metropolitan city which was the Federal Capital of Nigeria at the time; with no known relative. Even though I had two of my step-siblings living in the same city, since I had no relationship with them and did not even know how to contact them, he was the only person I knew. That night he told me he is aware I was pregnant and that revelation came as both a relief and a shock to me. He also told me that what his sister gave me was not to abort the pregnancy instead they were "vitamins" and he pulled out the bottle from his luggage. I told him what my mother had told me about abortions but at the same time, I was not sure how she will receive this news since I was not married. I knew that such a thing is seen as a taboo in our community and can be shameful to our family. He reassured me that he would travel back to consult with his parents about us getting married.

When I related the news to my mother it didn't go down well with her but was pleased that they did not support having the pregnancy aborted, insisting that she will not consent to any marriage until I graduate from the university and that I could stay with them till the baby is born.

All I kept thinking was how I was going to cope with a baby while overseas. That did not seem to be any problem at all like his mother and my mother both said they are available to care for the baby while we both pursue our educational careers overseas. My school Leaving Certificate

Result came result came and I passed with 5 credits which were enough to earn me entrance into the University. I could with such credits go on to become a Medical Doctor, Pharmacist, Engineer, or any other science-related career. He had good credits too but they were in the Arts, so we decided I was going to become a Medical Doctor while he will becomes a Lawyer.

The Birth of my baby

I gave birth to a baby boy, staying with his parents. Meanwhile, my godmother took a 12 monthly course to become a midwife, she met and got married to a businessman who was dealing in petroleum products with multiple gas stations. Meanwhile, her brother would visit twice a month, and I noticed that he stop talking about the furtherance of our education. Four months after the delivery of my first baby, I got pregnant again and it became so obvious that the plan of traveling abroad was a mirage as he was now seriously considering working for his sister's husband with plans to relocate to take up a manager's position in the business. That was when, it became obvious to me and my family that the possibility of my going back to school was under threat unless drastic action is taken, and his plan of traveling overseas was over.

Divine Intervention

On this fateful day, I came across a torn section of a local newspaper, picked it up, and read that the University of Benin was accepting applications for what they called Pre-Med School, and the minimum requirements were four-credit. Since I had 5, I kept the single sheet of paper and showed it to my mom when she visited. She in turn showed it to her brother who buys the local newspaper regularly and the full advertisement was seen. My mother brought it to me and told me to keep it a secret, while she went and submitted an application on my behalf with a copy of my credit score.

Six months into the second pregnancy, just before my first child turned a year, he had a high fever from infection and died before we could make it to the hospital.

Now or Never

Devastated from the loss of my first child and coupled with the fact that the man who made so many promises to me had reneged, my mother had an escape plan for me as soon as I delivered my second child. I also told my mum that he said I could go to a 12 monthly vocational program like his sister, but such a proposition was not acceptable as far as my mother was concerned even though my dad wanted to play along.

I put to bed a baby girl, and two days after I was discharged to go home. Before now, my mother had told the nurses not to tell his parents when I will be discharged so it was easy to plan my escape because at this time he was hardly around, spending a lot of time with the businessman. On the morning of my discharge, I sneaked out of the hospital knowing fully well that on weekdays, his mother would have gone to the local market and his father to work. I packed my belongings from his parents' house and headed back to the hospital, with a prearranged vehicle I was discharged with the newborn baby, and I went home with my mother.

It is My Fault! My mother would say it over and over

When we arrived at my mother's place, the atmosphere was un-imaginable. Except for my father who knew about what has transpired during the last 18-20 months, not even my step-mother knew, but because she was not on good terms with my mother she could not ask any questions.

However, I could tell from her premonitions by side comments like: "well there goes the all 'saints', 'the holier than Mary' with a baby outside wedlock". She knew the newborn baby was mine but couldn't ask the obvious question. My mother, on the other hand, would respond with great joy that "she thanks God that her daughter did not abort the baby and that she is now a grandmother"

Oh! How I wished the exchange of words would stop, or I wished I never met my godmother.

My daughter was named "Aromohelen" which means "when you are done playing with a child that does not belong to you, it is a must you return the child to the owner".

Every morning and evening when my mother gives the baby a bath she would pray over her that she is not a mistake or a hindrance but a blessing. Her name was a direct response to the insult, my step-mother, daily makes, telling her that "the father and family of my daughter did not reject me or her" and that my child was not a "bastard" and that instead, we chose not to stay in the relationship. My father was not too happy either but directed his anger toward my mother who encourage the relationship between me and my godmother saying it was my mother that permitted me to go spend the holidays with her.

Despite his anger, he was very caring and would always want to hold the baby, bring me treats, and would give me money to buy the baby's formula. Even though my baby was not his first grandchild but she was the very first he has seen and held, since both of my step-sisters had 4 children in total, two from each of them, but none of the 4 grandchildren has been seen by my father but only by my step-mother went to visit and cared for them after delivery according to tradition.

This brought about the question of why I was in my father's house with a baby instead of my mother visiting me in my husband's house to care for me after delivery? Again it was obvious that my mother and I have gone against the tradition, which created the speculation that my daughter must be a bastard and that I must have been so flirtatious that I did not know who must have impregnated me.

There were the stares, and disappointed looks, and few who were bold to ask who the father was, were promptly answered by my mum stating the father's name and family. She would further explain that she decided to bring me home. Even though that did not quite satisfy their curiosity the name given to my child gave the whole narrative away. I had a child outside wedlock, and though I was not the first it was very rare in our community, and those who did were scorned and seen as irresponsible; who found it difficult to find husbands, and so end up staying and spending the rest of their lives in their father's house.

Righting all the Wrongs

Having such an undeterred and persistent mother was all I could have asked for as my mother was relentless, insisting I must not let the hard work of earning such a good grades go to waste. When my daughter was three months old, I took the common entrance test to the University and passed. I attended the selection interview and was selected for the Pre-Med Program. This news had a bitter-sweet paradox to it because of the financial burden of attending university would be great on my parents.

But to my mother, this gave her great joy and she immediately change her narrative or story to "Oh she is taking care of my daughter so I could go to medical school". That did not come as a surprise since my academic achievement was well-publicized even in the local newspaper. Also at this time most of my classmates were already in their University of choice, so I was one year behind. My mother would always say God know it would take me a long time to finish and give her a grandchild, hence he made the provision now! Well, I never saw it from that perspective, instead, my buried shame and guilt, took on a different tone. How was I to face my fellow students at the university and tell them that I was already a mother at 18yrs outside wedlock? I had sleepless nights and cold feet as the days drew near for classes to begin.

As much as I could not wait to leave my father's house to escape the daily sarcastic side comments from my stepsister, I was also not oblivious that most within my age bracket at this time had traveled out of the village to cities or the Universities. The few at home were hardly seen since they too carried a different type of shame, yet culturally mine was seen and perceived as the worst kind of shame or disappointment to any family or household. At least they had good reason to be home since they could retake the School Leaving Certificate as external students; improve their credits and go on to attend a trade/

vocational school or the university. I could tell that some would wish I could transfer my credit to them so they could move on, as they considered my predicament a "waste" of my credits and time. Some girls my age knew so much about birth control while the naïve ones who got pregnant and tried to abort their pregnancy either ended up dying or had serious complications. Despite all the obvious, I was wretched with a thick layer of shame and guilt.

The Night Before

Preparing to go to college was a huge financial investment on the part of any parent as schools were not free. But with the help of my relentless mother, I was able to get the few items I needed and I was off to school leaving my 3-month-old baby with my mother to care for. At this time neither my godmother and her brother nor anyone from her family bothered to check on me and the baby as they were very upset that I went to my parents' house straight from the hospital.

My dad had not been paid for over three months and I had no idea how I was going to get the money I needed but the night before my departure for college, I was very depressed as the day rolled by, constantly looking out for my dad to walk him with some good news to no avail.

During dinner, I refused to eat despite my mother's pleas. She then told me to escort her to see someone she was waiting for at nightfall so no one would see or notice us. When we made it to a house which I did not recognize nor did I know any of the occupants, we knocked on the door and a lady about the age of my mother opened and told us to come in and have a seat. She went into her room, came back, and beckoned my mother to sit with her at a long wooden table with a flickering lantern. To my surprise, my mother un-tucked her wrapper and placed a white handkerchief on the table and I could hear the giggling sounds of what I believed were her pieces of jewelry (gold jewelry). As I watched with keen attention, I saw the woman bring out some items that looked like currency from a black bag, placed them on the table, and uttered some words I could not understand. After the transaction, I stood up to follow my mother out but the lady walked to me, stood before me, and said. "you better behave when you get to school". I understood what those coded words meant, so I replied yes mama. I knelt as a gesture of respect, thanking her but at the same time wondering if she knew that I was "already messed up". With a big smile on my mother's face and words of thanks and appreciation from my mother to the woman, we finally left.

I was greatly relieved even though I did not know the exact amount the woman gave my mother. I also did not bother to ask, instead, I followed in silence as she burst into spontaneous praise and thanks to God.

After a few turns here and there we made it to another house, my mother knocked and a man whom I recognized as the owner of a convenience store opened the door. Again I watched as my mother handed him some money and he gave her some bags with provisions (5 bags in all) which she handed to me. My mother had been at the man's store and chosen the items in the bag promising to come to retrieve them later. As if this was rehearsed, the man stepped up to me and wished me well in college saying he is so proud of me.

Once again in my head, I thought something was not right as I thought everyone knew what happened to me but that was not the case. I was now feeling very good when we left the man knowing I was going to school the next day.

My Uncle had bought me a big suitcase as a gift for college and now it was full of almost every item on the prospectus that the school issued. On getting home, my dad who was waiting did not need to ask how it went as it was obvious that things went well with the bags of provisions we brought in but I could tell he was very happy. That night, I could not sleep and stayed awake replaying the whole experience, particularly the fact that now my mother may or may never be able to retrieve those gold jewelry. I was afraid to ask if she had sold them or used them as collateral for a loan as the former was too painful to imagine so I did not bother to ask my mother even up to this day. I have no idea if she ever got to retrieve those pieces of jewelry.

About 10 am the next day, using a pre-arranged transport I departed for college with the utmost secrecy one could imagine. My siblings were involved in the scheme so two of them entered the taxi with me to appear as if they were the ones traveling and when nobody was paying attention, I hopped in and the taxi took off only to drop my two brothers a few blocks away so that they could walk home. I have no idea how long it took my stepmother and others to know that I was not around, because I was not usually seen outside with my baby, spending all day inside the house. I left with missed emotions thinking about how my mother would cope; how I would cope at school; so I decided I would hide this information as much as I could and that was exactly what I did. None of my classmates or friends knew I had a newborn baby outside wedlock. For whatever reason, my body did not give away my secrets so once again providence was at work.

My Confession of Faith – The Scripture Union (SU)

At the University there was a Christian Organization called "The Scripture Union" (SU) which was a well-respected students' faith-based organization. It had as its sole mission to encourage students to have only two goals while in college; firstly, a commitment to be a follower of Christ and the second a commitment to excel in their studies.

As was their customs, a welcome service was held on the school compound with a make-shift podium. I had never seen or been to such a program and the atmosphere was charged; the organizers were so joyful, singing, and dancing to worship songs and choruses most of which I never heard before. The good thing was that they were very simple that anyone could sing along. I had never seen people sweating so profusely with so much energy; it was so contagious that it was practically impossible to stand still and watch. Before I knew what was happening, I was dancing and singing along. I got lost in the joyful atmosphere that if you were there you would think, I have always been one of them. This continued till eventually, I saw a fair-skinned young man step onto the makeshift podium, took the microphone, and opened with Amen, Amen, and Amen!

The music slowly died down and he opened the bible he had and read some scriptures which I could not articulate as the voices around me kept shouting Hallelujah over and above what he was saying. Suddenly the young man stopped talking and asked us to all bow our heads in prayers. He prayed and began to make what I came to know as an "altar call" for salvation. I remember the exact word he spoke that day but one particular phrase stuck with me; he said "if you want to make it through this college and not waste the money, and all it took for your parents to send you here, you must make a choice today, right now to be born again so that Christ can help you succeed; come out now and give your life to Christ".

Immediately the whole scene of the night before flashed through my mind and the words of the woman who gave my mother the money echoed in my ears so loud that I ran out to the front where some students had all lined up to pray for anyone who would respond. As I made my way to the front, two female students met me and held my hands, and started to pray for me with such passion and fervency. I was later led to a quiet spot where they took my name, dormitory, and room number, and promised to check on me the next day which happened to be a Saturday.

As promised they showed up, and I followed them to a shade under a tree where they talked with me. They brought me a bible, and the relationship continued and from that time I never felt alone or lonely on the outside but inside I was still wracked with shame and guilt. I kept saying to myself if they only knew who I was and how I had made a mess of my life, they would be so disappointed, so I never told them about my past.

Being second and third-year students respectively, they took and treated me as a junior sister. In the Scripture Union, the members were there for each other. Whenever there is a lack the students all pulled resources together to help with provisions/clothes and shoes, and even with school fees. Some of the lecturers that were Christians were also supporting financially, and the Organization was known to set such a high standard morally and academically. As to be expected we were mocked and scorned by other students who see us as poor and anti-social but we were well respected for our academic performance because no SU member must be caught in any form of scandal, either examination or sexual. We were also accountable to each other, being each other's keepers with females pairing with females and males with males, calling each other brothers and sisters.

Career Change

When I went home for the holidays, my mother was doing a great job with my baby who was now walking and so adorable, but she told me that my dad had not been paid his retirement allowance for over 9 months and they are barely surviving. She has been praying that God will make a way for me to continue the next school year, and interjected by saying "Bose do not worry, you will go back to school next year". I had to encourage myself to be focused as I had final exams to write but I was almost thorn apart making it back to school with almost no provision. However, my worries were unfounded because my SU sisters helped me with some provisions.

On this fateful day, I was in the cafeteria and I saw a big poster pasted everywhere that the Federal Government of Nigeria was recruiting students to the School of Nursing attached to the Teaching Hospital with monthly allowances as incentives to solve the shortage of nurses the country was facing. I was immediately pulled to this offer, took the information, and applied, though I did not share this with anybody as I thought it was shameful for me to withdraw from pre-med to nursing due to financial constraints. I was overqualified as they only required a minimum of three credits two of which must be Biology and Chemistry or physic and I had 5 credits in the science subjects.

Behold, I was invited to a selection interview with a panel of 7 judges, as providence would have it, the interview site was in the Hospital's Conference Hall, and a walking distance also from our hostel. Since the interview was on a Saturday, I told my SU sisters that I will be visiting a relative in town and will see them later at the fellowship. On arriving at the interview center, I saw that some individuals were taking what looked like a test. Somehow I felt unprepared but as I presented my letter of invitation I was ushered to another section of the conference room and was asked to sit until I was called in. I met 5 others sitting and waiting to be called, one of them asked me how many credits I had, and I said "five" and she said "okay" because this is what excludes you from taking the test. I then breathe a sigh of relief and ask how many credits she have she had; she said "four, and that anyone with four and more credits who took all science subjects was exempted from the test". I said to myself so far so good.

Eventually, I was called to meet with the panel, and the first question was; "are you sure you want to change your career from pre-med to nursing" I was not prepared for such a question and I immediately said, "my mother had wanted me to be Nurse and I will love to grant her that desire", that was all I said and I was asked to sign some papers and expect a letter for a starting date the following year when school resumes.

As I was about to exit the door one of the panel members said "make sure you do not change your mind". I turned and with eye contact, shook my head and said, "Madam I will not change my mind". With a smile and a wave of hands to bid me goodbye, I exited the hall, walked silently to my room, and pondered what just happened. As I laid down flat on my back, I started to imagine myself in one of the nurses' white uniform with the color-coded belts and cap and also how my mother related to the nurses on the two occasions I was in the hospital. She had expressed the fact that she wished I would be a nurse- so here I was in the process of becoming one.

Again, I kept this information away from all, encouraged that at least I will be back to school next year and will still be able to participate in the SU activities since the School of Nursing and The University share the same acreage with the Schools of Pharmacy, Dentistry, Psychology, and Medicine utilizing the same Teaching Hospital that the School of Nursing uses. At least, I do not have to worry about school fees (all being paid by the

Federal Government). To crown it all I was going to be receiving a monthly allowance of 120 Naira for personal upkeep, to me this was a divine provision by the providential hand of God, and I could not be more right.

Chapter Eight

The Crux of the Matter

After 10 years of living in our house, we began to notice cracks on the wall right next to our bedroom closet. Initially, it didn't look really serious, it seemed like very small cracks here and there, nothing too serious. It was also situated on a part of the wall that was hardly noticeable, you had to look up and look hard to see it. So, my husband and I decided that it wasn't a problem. When I had my second child, my sister advised me to put a plaster over the cracks. It was a fairly simple task and it covered the cracks neatly. We thought we were rid of the problem but were shocked to realize a year later that the cracks had become bigger and more noticeable. We tried to stay calm for a few months until they became a bigger problem. These cracks were massive and went all the way to the ceiling of the house. We then realized that in our bid to give the initial problem a quick fix, we had neglected the role of professionals and had missed the real problem entirely – the foundation.

There are cracks in our lives and these cracks are of spiritual significance. The happiness we all desire is not something we can achieve by plastering over the cracks with our wisdom, strength, academic achievement, fat bank account, or relationships. We can only break through when we let go of ourselves and hand over the reins of our lives to God. I call this being 'carefully careless' with your life. God has to be the foundation, the very core of our success.

For 9 years, 3 months, and 22 days, the Lord took me through a process of understanding and internalizing the concept of the Proverbs 31 woman. The scripture describes her as a woman who 'intentionally dresses with strength, dignity, and smiles at the future with inner confidence'. A lot of people think that the lifestyle is unattainable but I can assure you that it is attainable and very real.

Through my personal experiences, God has taken me through this class and I can say with all certainty and humility that I am that woman. Dressed with strength and dignity and confidence in the future because of my faith in the power of my God. Whoever we enthrone in our hearts determines how we respond to life's challenges. It determines how we smile in the face of an uncertain tomorrow. The bedrock is the heart, which we can also term our soul (our intellect, emotions, and will) and the spirit. Remember that the bible says that out of the heart flows the issues of life. God is more interested in our intentions than our actions. Before we can show forth the glory of God, we need to intentionally accept Jesus Christ and enthrone him as Lord of our lives, focusing on him alone.

Our house had visible cracks which were just symptoms but the real problem was the unseen foundation. My heart was the foundation that needed repairs. For years, I had been suffering under the weight of ignorance, fear, taking God for granted, and pursuit of pleasures and riches, which left me exhausted and so stressed that I would have serious headaches daily. I kept 'plastering over the cracks, just going through the motions, going to church, and basically being a nominal Christian until God intervened. In His infinite mercies, he lifted me with his word and made me strong enough to withstand life's storms. With every new day, I see how God is making me a strong woman who is fearless in the face of uncertainty. Now that I think about it, the root of my dysfunctional lifestyle was Shame.

Shame and guilt

As a young girl, I was ashamed of the family I was born into. I remember sitting in the middle of the classroom to avoid my poor clothes being noticed. I also had no shoes so I would wait till the end of the class and sneak past the students. I remember the feeling of shame of knowing that my mother was married into a polygamous family because none of my classmates were from polygamous homes. I felt inadequate, not good enough, not worthy, unintelligent, powerless, or acceptable enough. I learned to show up wearing different personality masks hiding how I truly felt. Thank God for his word spoken through Paul to the Corinthians where we learn not to compare ourselves to others.

The word shame is used a lot in the bible and it also has different Hebrew root words. One of them is 'bwush' or 'boosh'. In English, it is written directly as 'blush' but it signifies thoughts of public humiliation, disillusionment, a broken spirit, and confusion. Other Hebrew words that mean shame, include 'kalam', 'Cherpah', 'kana', 'shimtash', 'shaman', 'Ervah', and 'chapher'.

"Kalam" means to wound, taunt, insult with the effect of causing shame, dishonor, or disgrace.

"cherpah" refers to rebuking, pointing the finger, or stigma. "kana" means to cause one to "bend the knee" to bring low, or to humble. "shimtash" means "scornful whispering" (of hostile spectators) to shame. "Shaman" refers to cause to grow numb, to devastate.

"Ervah" refers to nudity, nakedness, or shame. "chapher" alludes to the detection of the causes of shame.

These are the words used in the Hebrew version of the Old Testament. The New Testament which was written in Greek gives other words that do not add any other unique definition of shame so I will leave them out.

According to Webster's New World Dictionary, shame is defined as 'A painful feeling of having lost the respect of others because of improper behavior, incompetence, etc. of oneself or another; a tendency to have feelings of this kind or a capacity for such feelings.' It is also defined as dishonor or disgrace (to bring shame to one's family).

The college edition describes it as 'A painful emotion excited by a consciousness of guilt, shortcomings, or impropriety,' or 'susceptibility to such feelings or emotion.'

Suffice it to say that shame is an inner sickness or 'disease of the soul' that expresses itself through inner torments. The emotional torment that is associated with shame is based largely on an individual's thoughts about themselves whether they are true or not. It is deeply rooted in the ignorance of an individual of his or her potential and blessings. People usually say that what you do not know cannot hurt you, I disagree. What you don't know can hurt you just the way gravity affects you even if you don't know it exists.

It is very important to differentiate guilt from shame. The main distinction is that guilt always comes with an expectation of consequences because of something you've done or caused but shame doesn't always have an expectation of consequences. While shame comes from failing to live up to one's standards or society's standards (real or imagined), guilt comes from breaking those standards. Shame has no apparent remedy because it is A MINDSET ABOUT IDENTITY while guilt is A MINDSET ABOUT

MISTAKEN ACTIONS OR INACTIONS. The pain associated with guilt is predicated on one's actions and deeds while the pain associated with shame is predicated on one's understanding of their identity, nature, worth, core personality, and their essence.

GUILT IS FOR MAKING A MISTAKE, SHAME IS FOR BEING THE MISTAKE. If a person makes a mistake, it may be possible to rectify it but if a person believes that he or she is a mistake, there are no obvious solutions to that. It would take something divine to restore that person, a total spiritual rebirth and renewal.

Shame differs from most emotions, in that, it is learned. We tend to learn it early on through actions directed at us or words spoken to us in our families and communities. Unfortunately, once you begin to learn it, it takes hold of your subconscious and begins to define your very existence. You begin to internalize it as a perfect emotional response to most situations and it sets the tone for your interaction with the world.

A lot of believers have developed 'Churchy clichés' to mask their feelings of shame and inadequacy about themselves and their past. They should remember that God never makes junk. Everything He made is for a purpose! He deliberately decides when and where a person is born, which family he is born into, and everything that becomes material or real about that person. He doesn't create mistakes.

However, it takes the light of God to shine over all the dark paths of lies and make the truth known. Isaiah 62:21 says 'thy people also shall be all righteous: they shall inherit the land forever, the branch of my planting, the work of my hands, that I may be glorified.' Isaiah 61:3 says

> "To appoint unto them that mourn in Zion, to give unto them beauty for ashes, the oil of joy for mourning, the garment of praise for the spirit of heaviness; that they might be called trees of righteousness, the planting of the LORD, that He might be glorified."

You might not think that you were born into the wrong family, it might just be about the fact that you are too tall or too short, too fat or too slim. You might feel like you do not have a great nose, good teeth, curves, hair texture, eye color, and even skin color but remember that God NEVER makes mistakes so you are not a mistake.

Consider what is said about you in the book of Isaiah to be true. Whether you consider yourself a branch or a tree, a flower or a bush, you are the LORD's planting, that He might be glorified. The worth of a thing is determined by how much people are willing to pay for it. Jesus decided that you were precious and special enough to die for, so know your worth and glorify God every day. 1 Corinthians 6:20 says

> "For, ye are bought with a price: therefore, glorify God in your body, and in your spirit, which is God's."

Every one of us has experienced shame and embarrassment at some point in our lives. This has been passed down to us from the foundation of the earth and the time of Adam. I call this the 'fact' of sin which leaves us with the propensity, urge or desire to sin. I call this the 'fault' of sin.

In my case, believing that I was born into the wrong family led me to sin in my thoughts and actions (fault of sin). The Fault of Sin can also be identified in people if we trace their childhood, relationships with their spouses, families, and friends. There's no sudden action, it is always caused by something.

Shame can also be caused by disappointment or discontent with your society, the nation you come from, and your moral and ancestral heritage. This shame is usually collectivist. When one child causes his or her team to fail at a team sport, all the children tend to be ashamed of their performance and when a man or woman has an alcohol or drug addiction, even if they forget about it, their families tend to be ashamed of and for them. There are a lot of wives and children who are in the trap of shame by association because the father or husband tends to do the wrong things or has a publicly known addiction, even when no one says it out loud.

There is also the shame associated with work or performance. A lot of people tend to judge their self-worth by the standard or perceived standard of their work. So, if you criticize such a person's work, it leads them to lose their self-confidence and live with a mindset of shame. For these people, a failure at their job means that they are failures as people. Objectivity goes out the window and their emotions push them to the brink, not being able to distinguish work from self. This is a very dangerous trajectory to be on. Truth is, just as the devil lied to me about my self-worth and my family's worth, he lies to these people as well and they believe it.

Satan is great at making us play his game. He makes us question God, torments us constantly about every step we take, and constantly makes us doubt ourselves. He denies us peace by making us feel unworthy, unloved, unimportant, and fleeting which prevents us from living our God-given lives in the abundance that He has provided us. If we are not careful, we could lose ourselves in this spiral and ultimately lose our lives.

The first step to attaining freedom from shame is to IDENTIFY the root cause of your shame. If you have not identified it, then you cannot confront it and if you have not confronted it, then you can never conquer it.

Two roots of shame

There are broadly two roots of shame; one is based on a collective, societal or national feeling while the other is individual.

Collective shame comes from carrying out unrighteous acts (Obadiah 1:10-15), acts of mockery of God (2 Chronicle 32:10-13), and groups of people attacking or persecuting God's anointed. (Psalms 4: 1-2, 31:17, 35:4, 25-26, 40:14-15).

Individual shame comes from acts of nudity (Exodus 32:25) bad behavior of a Parent (1 Samuel 20:33-34) sexual assault or abuse (2 Samuel 13:4-13), foolish behavior (Proverbs 9:7), laziness (Proverbs 10:5), pride or haughtiness (Proverbs 11:2, 16:18, Matthew 23:12), wickedness (Proverbs 13:5), refusal to receive instruction or correction (Proverbs 13:18) presumption (Proverbs 18: 13, 25: 8), dishonoring parents (Proverbs 19: 26, Ephesians 6:2-3), gossip and revealing of secrets (Proverbs 25: 9-10).

There's a striking similarity between the two. Psychiatrists believe that shame is the underlying symptom of most psychological disorders. Shame can be seen at the very base of rebellious attitudes which is manifested when someone is told to do something that they don't want to do or that they cannot do. These things are usually felt to be beneath them or undignified. Rejection, inferiority complex, and depression all have shame as their common factor. It tells you that you are no good, defective, or inferior, leaving you feeling hopeless and hopelessness always leads to depression.

The onset of shame

Emotions are a gift from God, they occur naturally and are usually instinctive. There are two classes of emotions; primary and secondary emotions. Primary emotions are the ones you are born with like anger, happiness, frustration, fatigue, discomfort, fear, joy, and love. These emotions are present even before a child develops self-awareness. Secondary emotions are developed as a child becomes more self-aware and conscious of their emotions. Some of them are pride, guilt, embarrassment, and self-consciousness.

Shame is developed before guilt. A child learns to blush even when they are not yet self-aware, even before they understand the concept of right and wrong. As we grow older, shame comes from our failures in keeping God's commands and following his instructions which strain our relationship with Him. As was the case with Adam and Eve, sin is an obvious source of shame. When they sinned, they hid from God because they were naked and ashamed. (Genesis 3:7).

Unfortunately, we now have new and strange teachings that say there is no good or evil, no right or wrong. Such people do not want to contend with the fact that they are accountable to God. So, they use denial as a way to mask their shame and their fear of facing God and heaven.

Parents also have had a hand in inducing shame among children whether consciously or unconsciously, creating a shame-prone environment in the way they discipline their children. I'm sure you've heard words like 'shame on you' used on children with disorderly conduct. Some parents use this statement as a means of correcting their children thereby laying the foundations for a shame-based life. Shame can also be passed on by parents unknowingly through their mannerisms and noticeable attitudes. My parents did not get married according to the societal norms at the time and as such, I constantly felt a sense of despair knowing that I would be disregarded by people based on my parents' decisions. Nowadays, there are all sorts of parental behaviors for children to be ashamed about. Parents engaging in extra-material affairs, watching or participating in adult movies or videos, fighting or domestic violence, declaring a change in sexual orientation or gender identity, and many more. The painful part is watching the children who are affected by their parents' actions suffer ridicule and shame because of their parents' immoral choices.

The devil always creates a false sense of shame and tries to torment you by telling you that you are either immoral by your actions or immoral by association. He peddles lies that tell you that you have done something wrong and thus should be ashamed of yourself. He tells you 'Shame on you but you have a choice to either accept or reject his lies. Demonic and Spiritual shame can be linked to traumatic and sinful experiences through association or learning.

Imagine being in an auto crash, you might develop a fear of driving. Alternatively, if you lost a father or mother to an automobile crash, you might inherit the fear of driving from the experience of your parents. We tend to fear things and then project those fears on others. 'Watch out for that car, it might hit you…' this is a clear projection of one's feelings about cars that can bring fear of driving to someone else. So, as much as one can be raised in a fear-driven world, there are also parents who raise their children in shame-ridden conditions. Unconsciously, these kids are taught to be extremely strong people. Unfortunately, parents have used shame as an effective tool for exercising control over their children. Statements like "if you love me, you will…" or "if you are a good son/daughter you will…" so the parents will not be shamed, is a commonly used tactic.

An example of this is when a parent disapproves of a child's behavior and expresses this to the child, implying or even stating shame for that behavior. The child desiring to restore fellowship with the parent(s), modifies or changes his or her behavior. However, the child (especially so in the case of older children) gives up some portion of his or herself (soul) to impress or accommodate the parent(s). This might be fine where the required behavioral change is good and very necessary for the child's safety. Examples of such comments are 'Don't go out in the street alone' and 'I will tell your dad when he gets home from work'.

Consequently, when a child is shamed by parents, affinity is broken and the child feels abandoned. To re-establish that connection with the parents, the child begins to seek approval by trying to be perfect.

Interestingly, shame is considered by some psychologists to be beneficial and instructive, as a means of controlling social behavior. This is very strange and unscriptural. As a believer, I know that there are better ways of correcting or redirecting behavior. The godly discipline of a child is a form of deliverance and the book of Proverbs addresses this in great detail. Unscriptural discipline like when the child is forced to sit in a corner, wear a 'dunce's cap' at school, and 'time out' at home are ways of shaming a child into socially acceptable behavior. Yet each act is a form of abandonment and not only shames the child but reinforces the feeling of abandonment that may already be present.

Sadly, the one who has been controlled by shame usually will attempt to manipulate others with shame. This is the classic effect of traditional witchcraft. In the sense that the one controlled usually winds up controlling others, in the same way, he or she was controlled. Victims of being judged usually become judgmental to others and will exhibit a Critical Spirit. Such individuals are also plagued by the comments of others and can end up depressed and introverted. Using shame to control behavior is not unlike spiritual witchcraft. Since witchcraft is defined as manipulation, control, domination, and attempting to get others to do your will by channeling the power of a spirit that is not godly.

Even in something like prostitution, shame is at the root. When a person believes that giving away the body is the easiest way to gain the acceptance and approval of others. This causes a stifling of the individual's personality and the assumption of a false personality that is appealing to others. Shame is often the root of this behavior. Imagine the level of greatness we could demonstrate by living to the fullness of our true personalities as God's children.

For shame involving sexual abuse of a child, the child tends to disassociate herself or himself, and their true personality is shattered. Shame is introduced by the child's feelings of wrongdoing or failure and is usually a tool used by the offending party to rationalize their sin. Many children who have suffered sexual abuse feel ashamed of themselves and sometimes think they are responsible for what they have gone through.

A good example of societal shame, collective ridicule, and public humiliation played out when the Jews were made to wear the Yellow Star of David by Nazi Germany to shame them.

Unfortunately, society today facilitates the effects of shame through acts of discrimination and by judging certain persons or groups to be defective, inferior, or outsiders. The people who are being judged experience shame for non-conformity to the perceived societal standard. This is seen across racial, socio-economic, and ethnic lines. Shame and anger can also be taught to a child by an adult who lived through more difficult and turbulent times. This is the case with children who feel shame and inferiority related to their ancestors having been slaves. Often, anger and bitterness are present when a person is repeatedly taught about racial abuse. The presence of shame and anger can do great harm and stifle the peace and joy of the Holy Spirit. On the other hand, love, and forgiveness, can cover a multitude of sins, bringing healing and inner freedom.

There's also a type of shame that I call 'in the box shame and guilt' which particularly affect people of color who lived in constant fear because they have been told that the white man hates them and is trying to kill them by throwing dynamite into their churches or even their homes. Some African American people experienced these evil acts and this led majority to live in perpetual fear and also pass the same to their children. Regrettably, some churches and some so-called ministers make a living out of exploiting the fear of people, even at a time when these occurrences are highly unlikely. For too long men have turned the people of God into some sort of merchandise, serving their ends. May God have mercy on them!

Truly, some people still lump others into stereotypical categories and label them with ethnic slurs. We have grown up in a society where every ethnic group has a stigma or slur of some kind and this could also be compounded by the other forms of shame that an individual can suffer. Perhaps this is the result of the United States being the 'Great Melting Pot' with huge cultural differences still seen today among different ethnicities, especially in large cities like Houston, Texas where I reside. I remember hearing one person of color telling another person of color, 'Go back to your country!' There are also other shame-causing phrases in our society, such as the label attached to certain children by their schools when they have some challenges with learning. Tags like ADD, slow-learner, poor student, and a variety of others. Curses such as, 'You will never learn mathematics', 'You will never be able to hold a job', 'You are not smart enough to go to college' also build negativity. The painful thing is that the ones so stigmatized usually believe those lies and thereby limit themselves from becoming all they are capable of being.

I heard a quote by the comedian George Globel, 'I feel like brown shoes in a tuxedo world,' implying that he did not feel like he fits in anywhere and for a long time I felt like that until God liberated me.

There are some arbitrary societal rules and standards that cause people to experience shame. In some parts of the world, not burping after a meal is considered discourteous and a source of shame for the host meaning the meal was not satisfying but in the west burping is discourteous. Families, parents, churches, cultures, and societies have all used shame one way or the other to control the behavior of others.

There is also societal shame at birth when a woman conceived out of wedlock or got married to someone as a single mother and does not tell the child that her current husband is not his or her biological father. Tragically, the biological father may not even know he has a child and sometimes dies before the full story is revealed. This can lead to shame for the child and everyone else directly involved. This reminds me of Jeremiah 20:18 where he implied that he inherited the spirit of shame from the womb.

Consider a single-parent home, where the male child is expected to assume the role of husband/ father, which invariably creates a sense of shame due to being inadequate and overwhelmed by the expectation placed on such a young child. This is very common between the single mother and a son, where the son is shamed for his inability to meet needs and shame of comparing his home to others.

In some societies, certain behaviors are considered shameful like a boy and girl holding hands or a married lady shaking hands with a man, not her husband. So when a child nurtured in such a society finds himself or herself in an environment where such behavior is culturally acceptable, the child feels ashamed.

Shame can make us so vulnerable to control by others, especially those with Jezebel spirit. The devil knows all our weaknesses and vulnerable spots. He knows our 'hot buttons'. I believe that this is one of the causes of homosexual behavior. Those who had their single mother, grandmother, or aunt's voices so predominant in their formative years, express a strong feminine spirit which greatly adds to their shame.

The shame-plagued person is insecure, and their self-confidence and self-worth are easily destroyed. Shame devours self-confidence like the roaring lion in the Bible. It works hand-in-hand with pride to oppress an individual and to gain a foothold in the psyche preventing any opportunity of finding help. It always cripples and hinders the one living in it. It must be confronted and dealt with spiritually before it destroys a person's masculinity or femininity, and confidence, and ultimately takes one's life.

We need to be careful not to confuse shame with embarrassment. Embarrassment is caused by some action or mistake which is considered to be relatively unimportant and outside oneself. For example, spilling a beverage at a dinner party perhaps due to being clumsy or not particularly paying attention may cause an individual to be embarrassed but their self-worth is not threatened. Shame is more detrimental to a person's life. In a grade school, a boy had a bad experience of being shamed while attempting to ask a girl out through the phone. Because of the shame that he felt, he completely froze and refused to call any other girl on the phone. This phobia was so real that in college, he would either wait to be called by girls to college dance dates and other functions, or he would wait till he sees the girl in person to have a conversation. He was still single, even in his sixties just because he could never get over his grade school shaming experience.

The effects of shame and embarrassment are particularly related to a person's personality and upbringing. If you are raised in a home where you were taught not to take yourself too seriously, you will probably be able to avoid shame but if you have the spirit of shame already in place, even the minor embarrassment of the spilled beverages can be internalized as shameful. Shame not only affects the individual, but it affects everyone that is associated with that individual. When shame has its roots in a person, it produces fruits in that individual's life and the lives of those around him.

For example, children born out of wedlock may lie to cover the shame they feel. They could also try either avoiding such conversation or making up stories about their wonderful parents. Again, we must remember that Satan the father of all lies is behind this and he doesn't just cause them to lie but also causes them to feel guilty afterward.

Fruits of shame

People react differently in varying situations and circumstances. Even identical twins born and raised together could react differently to shame. One may be shame prone while the other may not because shame has a lot to do with what is going on inside the individual. No two individuals are the same. Some of us have been unfairly punished, and treated unjustly, so our reaction to being treated unfairly in the future may be much more painful and deeply felt. Some people become hardened by their painful experiences while others instead become timid, or fearful. Shame and rejection may cause one individual to accept the unjust treatment as deserving while another individual becomes angry, sometimes seeking revenge.

Children can begin at an early age to lie or tell half-truths, to avoid answering the question of a parent, especially when the child anticipates that the parent will react negatively (or that the answer will result in shame and rejection). Some fear that they will be abandoned if they are not perfect. The fear of abandonment is activated when one feels that they are defective, inadequate, or not up to the perceived standard. That shame-plagued individual believes that people can see nothing good in them and that everyone is focused on their flaws. This becomes an all-consuming issue in the individual's life and causes the individual to hide, conceal, isolate, and avoid any further chance of exposure to that painful feeling of inadequacy. This form of terror is experienced by those fearing abandonment.

There is a close connection between shame and the fear of abandonment. Both, focus on an expectation or fear that a person is going to be rejected often for some reason that he or she cannot understand. There is usually a feeling of dread, which can quickly become a panic. This kind of fear seems to be irrational.

As it is with shame, abandonment may either be due to rational or irrational fear. Certainly, all fear is irrational to some degree for Christians. In speaking of the rational aspect of the fear of abandonment, this is usually fear based on facts in the victim's past such as being abandoned by a parent or parents, the death of a parent, or a similar traumatic event that created an expectation of being abandoned. Sometimes this fear may be irrational; the victim or individual is unable to recall or remember any type of precipitating event or they exaggerate the event beyond what transpired. The most puzzling situations are those where the person happens to be physically and socially attractive. Outwardly, there is nothing "wrong" with them so there seems to be no basis at all for the fear. However, if one is a victim of shame-related fear of abandonment, they feel that they deserve to be abandoned because they believe that they are defective.

Mental function

People experiencing shame tend to shut down mentally, much as drunk people do, and they have difficulty accepting or processing what is being said to them. When a person is drunk, you cannot give them good advice.

Even if the advice is life-changing, it does the person no good, it is like telling someone hungry to stop thinking about food, or someone experiencing an irrational fear that there is nothing to fear.

Isolation

Shame disconnects us from others, even from God. That was the case with Adam and Eve in the book of Genesis. The shamed individual feels isolated and is shut off from everyone and that is exactly what the enemy wants. It gets even worse when the individual shuts himself or herself off from everyone who might be able to help, support or offer acceptance. The common trend is the individual burying the shameful experience deep subconsciously because they do not want to relive the pain of such a traumatic occurrence again. They would rather keep that part of their life secret and cover it up with diversions which may include outbursts of rage when there is a threat that their secret might be exposed. If the root is identified or threatened, the victim lashes out in what appears to be the offensive rage but in reality, is a defensive response. Note that rage like shame is all-encompassing. It can also literally take over the individual and cause them to become oblivious of everything around them.

Self-worth

Shame isolates an individual and causes them to question their self-worth. It can become a mental issue. It makes them say 'Everyone will hate me for what I have done or said. This is a black hole in which fear dwells. If the shame is felt and permitted its requisite secrecy, it grows and festers. Bringing the light of the Holy Spirit to bear upon it, by sharing it with a trusted, caring, non-judgmental person and exposing the issue with prayer, is the only thing that can free the individual. The only thing that can dispel darkness is light. The Light of the Holy Spirit can dispel the darkness of shame and its attendant, fear.

Spiritual and physical liberty

Shame is a spiritual issue and must be addressed accordingly. This is true in tackling its manifestations that sometimes lead to self-destructive behavior. The victim feels undeserving or unworthy of life which can spiral and that can be a precursor to 'spiritual' suicide; where this individual feels cut off from God because of their perceived defects and so they begin to die spiritually. Note that all spiritual issues always have physical repercussions. Usually, spiritual death could lead to physical death and if it is not countered with prompt loving intervention, the shamed victim begins a journey towards physical suicide.

Shame is destructive. Could it be that those who committed suicide during the great depression were just too ashamed to admit to their families, friends, and associates that they had lost everything they invested and could not imagine the prospect of begging or being considered poor?

Shame works like cancer, eating you up slowly from the inside, and is a prerequisite for depression and actual suicide. The shamed individual feels inadequate and defective, and depression sets in leading to spiritual suicide.

Emotional instability

Imagine the case of a wealthy businessman who is in a mental institution because the IRS serves him notice requesting his tax record, threatening to take his home and impound his business. He becomes so ashamed because his identity is directly tied to his wealth or social status, that it drove him mad. That's how far shame can drive a person's life when they become obsessed with what others think about them.

Others might resort to building a brash and controlling personality which is always on the defensive to 'control their narrative and protect them from shame and exposure. They cannot face the monster and so they avoid it at all costs.

Social phobia

In a social gathering, a shamed individual may feel so detached from what they perceive 'normal' people to be that they reduce their interaction with others. This is called a 'social phobia'- nervousness around others–a fear of shame and rejection based on what one perceived to be the unacceptability of their true selves. Consider a high school student who was ashamed of being in public because he had been born with a long nose. He would not go out on dates and hated attending classes because he believed he was disfigured. I believe that this could have been fixed by proper self-esteem teachings when he was much younger.

Self-focus

Shame at its roots is very diabolical in that it focuses on the self, causing the victim to become extremely self-centered. Yet, at the same time, it also seeks to destroy the self by isolating it from others and God. The ashamed individual tends to be too self-focused. The person who is either entirely, or primarily, self-focused is absorbed with his or her issues and problems so much so that a relatively minor problem such as losing car keys gets blown out of proportion. When this sudden, loud, and public raging subsides, they then try to be invisible, to escape or hide and will be found beating themselves up for weeks over perceived failure. Why? Because the shame and abandonment-plagued individuals feel that this is proof of their lack of worth. It looks to them to be another failure to attain perfection. Any perceived failure is a source of self-shame causing anger, fear, and torment. They sometimes make statements like 'I hate myself.

Science versus divine intervention

One of the bad fruits of shame is over-analyzing one's actions or motivations. This is common with those who have visited a psychologist, the individual believes by repeating or rehearsing their symptoms, others will accept them as being defective. Shame is spiritual and must be handled accordingly.

Disassociation

With shame comes a commonly observed defense mechanism: disassociation. When disassociation occurs, there is a shutting down of our God-given inner reassurance and a shutdown of all memory connections, especially those experiences which are too painful for the individual to bear such as a child undergoing sexual abuse, witnessing a murder, or seeing a loved one being burned to death. Disassociation, disconnecting, or blanking out may occur when life experiences are considered too painful to accept, or when memories are just too painful to be faced or retained. The mind of the person tries to simply blank out the memory. Not only is the person unable to remember much of what occurred, but certain other situations or people in their lives that might force them to relive the pain are also blocked out.

There is a similar effect to that of shock treatment, where entire segments of one's life may be blanked out of memory. The person eventually disassociates himself or herself from the past and abandons the present painful situation. For such people, normalcy can be lovingly restored by praying for them.

Starvation and Addiction

The shame-tormented individual is emotionally starved and suffers from a condition much like emotional anorexia (a loss of appetite for food). If allowed to fully run its course, shame will destroy its victim, because the individual is isolated from healthy human contact by his perceived torments. He is like a drowning victim gasping for air and seeks to find a means of filling the tremendous void created by the feeling of shame. The resulting action most of the time is to fall into an addiction of some sort.

Three categories of addiction are shame-related; Alcoholism, Perfectionism, and Work-a-holism.

Alcoholism

Alcoholism is perhaps the most common and most obvious. The Alcoholic is always burdened with shame, despair, self-hate, and disgust. It is also often difficult to determine whether the individual drinks because of shame or is ashamed because of the drinking. The truth is that there is always a hint of shame in alcoholism. A husband who feels or senses that his wife does not love him and that he is not the proper head of his household can get into drinking.

More specifically, alcoholics often suffer from a lack of relationship with a father figure. Many adult males talk about their lifelong search for a father. Never being able to find a father who loves and accepts them gives them an excuse to drink. Many alcoholics are intimidated by men. The void of a father figure can cause them to take one of two extremes: to develop a fear of men or to develop an unhealthy vulnerability towards homosexuality.

Marital issues and divorce are common causes of alcoholism. Feeling different, or being made to feel different, is a major tool employed by the enemy to isolate and torment individuals. He plays upon the vulnerability of the victim, telling them that they are not loveable and they are abnormal. That feeling of not being fulfilled as a man causes them to be extremely angry and violent when drunk. Interestingly, the intoxicated are more likely to fight, prove their sexual prowess or attempt some dangerous action they would never have attempted when sober.

Perfectionism

Both children and adults are victims of the myth of perfectionism. The shame-ridden adult, like the child, is driven to pursue perfection to win approval from various people; parents, teachers, spiritual leaders, or even an absent parent (living or dead). Sometimes it is an authority figure from the past who has shamed the victim.

Whatever the source of shame, the individual simply believes that he or she must do better or try to be perfect, if he or she is to be accepted. Most of the actions to overcome barriers or meet standards might be based on completely made-up ideals by the individual but has at its core the winning of approval becoming a major force in their life. Note that the standards we set for ourselves are often impossible to attain. This is especially the case with those standards imposed on us from the past. We need to start telling ourselves the truth, we cannot change the past, no matter how hard we try.

Work-a-holism

The workaholic is attempting to compensate for the void that shame has created in his or her life by working harder. He or she, is working to win someone's approval, to be successful among their peers, or to prove themselves to a boss, contemporary, or family. Instead of escaping into alcohol, he escapes into his work. His job comes as his source of solace. As noted, the alcoholic justifies their drinking with negative reasons. The workaholic, however, justifies his overworking for positive, even noble reasons; 'I am working hard to support my family,' 'We need the money,' 'I have to get ahead,' and many more. He seeks to justify his worthiness by working, although somewhere down deep he realizes that it is a high price for acceptance. This high price includes sacrificing their family/married life, and sometimes even health and peace.

Tragically, many individuals have tried to find escape via addictions, pornography, sex, food, alcohol, drugs, or to prove themselves through perfectionism. This is all to hide or escape from the painful reality of their shame. All these avenues only serve to increase their shame and torment.

The power behind the spirit of shame

The following are the spirits that dominate the individual with shame: the spirit of inferiority, the spirit of self-protection and control, the spirit of competition, the spirit of rejection, the spirit of self-focus, the spirit of social fear, the spirit of sexual guilt and spirit of other types of fear.

The spirits behind shame are commonly caused by parents or ancestral sins such as incest, alcoholism, and adultery. The spirit of inferiority commonly manifests fruits like condemnation, confusion, embarrassment, incompetence, and unworthiness. The spirit of self-protection and control manifests fruits such as ego, pride, vanity, self-righteousness, haughtiness, importance, arrogance, perfectionism, and manipulation. It might look out of place to list pride and vanity as fruits of shame but it is related in this case. An individual can be tormented with shame and hear the spirit of pride telling him 'You don't deserve to be treated like this.' 'You are better than those criticizing you because you are smarter, better educated, and more religious than them.' This spirit can become prevalent if unchecked.

The individual's desire to control or manipulate others eventually leads them to get involved in cult activities. The spirit of rebellion and anger manifests as criticism, frustration, irritability, intolerance, and resentment. The spirit of competition and self-protective spirit seems to have similar manifestations namely envy, jealousy, competition, and comparison. The spirit of rejection has the following fruits: self-rejection, self-condemnation, feeling unloved, feeling unwanted, feeling unaccepted, and abandonment.

It is important to note that demons desire to have their nature manifested in the individual they possess. The individual with a spirit of rejection does not immediately give room to the spirit to fulfill its mission, there must always be a situation that triggers the spirit to take prominence. The spirit of rejection invariably invites along with it an 'a rejection causing' spirit and they work hand in hand. For example, a rejection-causing Demon will have someone say words like 'Wow, you shouldn't wear plaid with that body type,' body-shaming the individual to trigger the spirit of rejection. Even if no words are used, the demon can say to the individual 'did you see the way they looked at you? They think you look stupid. This triggers the spirit of rejection.

The spirit of self or self-focus demons wants to keep the entire focus of life on oneself. The more self-focused we are, the less God-focused we are, and the less focus we place on others. This invariably will have a great impact on our ability and willingness to minister to others. Self-awareness, self-consciousness, over-sensitivity, regrets, and self-reproach are all fruits that this spirit manifests.

The spirit of social fear manifests itself in: blushing, confusion, incoherence, forgetfulness, blanking out, perspiration, and stuttering. The spirit of sexual guilt manifests itself in abortion, adultery, bestiality, early sexual experimentation, fornication, homosexuality, lesbianism, incest, lust, fantasy, masturbation, molestation, pornography, etc.

The spirit of fear manifests as the fear of humiliation, appearing stupid, being called out in public, being the center of attention, being made a spectacle, disgrace, inferiority, inadequacy, incompetence, rejection, making a fool of oneself, condemnation, criticism, failing God, embarrassment, failure, disappointment, accusation, dying, loss of respect, loss of reputation, public speaking (a recent survey shows that fear of speaking in public is the number one fear for most people)

Shame is the vehicle that carries all other harmful spirits. Working together with these spirits, this root spirit seeks to push an individual's personality out of balance. Thank God that there is a solution in His word.

It is important to observe that after Adam and Eve fell, God clothed and covered them so that no portion of their physical beings were legitimately exposed to the accusation of Satan. If the covering God provided for Adam and Eve with animal skin was adequate, how much more efficient is our better covering with the precious blood of Jesus? Satan no longer has any legal right to condemn us. Once we become partakers of and covered with the righteousness of Jesus, we are transported to the New Testament perspective. Even more significantly, we are comforted by the fact that Jesus Christ personally experienced shame at every level imaginable and therefore understands our suffering and associated shame.

These words in Isaiah 50:6-7 capture his suffering well:

> "I gave my back to the smiters, and my cheeks to them that plucked off the hair; I hid not my face from shame and spitting. For the Lord God will help me; therefore,

shall I not be confounded: therefore, have
I set my face like a flint, and I know that I
shall not be ashamed."

We can see that Jesus willfully chose to accept His death at the hands of sinful men' without a word of complaint. He willfully determined not to hide from shame or spite, as he easily could have done. Rather, He chose to pay the price of shame in full for us all, just as he did for sin and sickness. To be freed from shame, we must make Jesus our focus. According to Hebrew 12:2:

"Looking unto Jesus the author and finisher
of our faith, who for the joy set before Him,
endure the cross, despising the SHAME,
(perceived disgrace) and is sat down at the
right hand of the throne of God."

We know that Jesus believed in the love of God His father and that God had a good plan in store for Him. He did not, therefore, shrink from the shame of dying a criminal's death upon the cross. Instead, He continued obeying God to the best of His ability. As some translations rendered it, He 'disregarded the shame'.

The bearing of shame was an integral part of Jesus's crucifixion as seen in Hebrews 6:6 which speaks of causing Christ's shame in a warning. This verse warns that if one should fall away after having the full knowledge and acceptance of all Jesus was, and all that He accomplished on the cross, it would be impossible to renew them again 'to repentance'. They would have 're-crucified' the son of God, and 'put Him (again) to shame'. The Greek word employed here is *paradeig-matizo* which carries the thought of Christ being made a public spectacle, exposed to infamy, and openly shamed. We were also told that Jesus made himself of no reputation; He was willing to choose obedience to God over personal dignity. This is a characteristic we would do well to emulate. We have an audience of one, God, and He is the only person we need to please in this life therefore we don't need to be afraid or be overly concerned with people's opinions. This is truly easier said than done because we all clamor for affirmation one way or the way but by the grace of God we can do it.

Jesus was cruelly shamed and mocked upon the cross where He bore our shame and paid for the sins of Adam as well as our own. This narrative in Matthew 27:27-31, 35 paints a vivid picture:

> "Then the soldiers of the governor took Jesus into the common hall and gathered unto Him the whole band of soldiers, and they stripped Him and put on Him a scarlet robe. And when they had plaited a crown of thorns, they put it upon His head, and a reed in His right hand: and

they bowed the knee before Him, and mocked Him, saying "Hail King of the Jews!" And they spit upon Him, and took the reed, and smote Him on the head. And after that they had mocked Him, they took the robe off from Him, and put His raiment on Him, and led Him away to crucify Him. And they crucified Him, and parted His garments, casting lots: that it might be fulfilled which was spoken by the prophet, they parted my garments among them and upon my vesture did they cast lots".

Although they mocked Jesus and put a robe of scarlet upon Him (reminiscent of shame associated with the scarlet letter mentioned earlier), they could find no sin in Him because He already wore, in the spirit realm, a white robe of righteousness. We are also reminded that God has promised that 'though our sins are as red as scarlet, they shall be as white as snow.' Notice the complete perfection of God's provision for shame: Jesus was stripped naked and exposed to public humiliation three times before His actual crucifixion. The soldier stripped Him twice, once to put on Him the robe of mockery, and then after they abused Him, they removed that robe to replace His clothing. He was stripped naked again for the third time in preparation for the cross when they took His garments to gamble for them.

The crucifixion itself was not merely a means of execution, but also a means of public shame, as evidenced by the nakedness, and the placement of the crosses near the crossroads where all travelers could see the victims. So public and universal was the shame which Jesus bore that it had to be labeled in three languages. I pray that we do not miss the truth of all this verse: "Jesus bore our shame upon the cross. He did a complete and perfect work without complaint; He bore His shame and disgrace as well as our shame and disgrace, even to the point of suffering as a common criminal and dying a criminal's death. He bore the personal shame and disgrace of having His naked, scarred, bleeding body elevated on public display to be humiliated at a public thoroughfare. I hope we do not become sanitized by the artwork we are familiar with nowadays. It was not a comfortable scene as He hung upon that rugged cross. He was naked and broken, without a strip of clothing to cover Him.

It is pertinent to note that no matter the shame, disgrace, or embarrassment you feel you have undergone or are currently going through, Jesus not only understands but has already borne it and made provision for your healing and ultimate deliverance. Jesus has clearly expressed His will for us to be free from every vestige of shame–in the same way, that He has expressed His will for us to be free from sin and sickness–by His death upon the cross. He willingly died to pay the full price for all our sins, our guilt, our sicknesses, and our shame.

1 John 1:7

> 'But if we walk in the light, as He is in the light, we have fellowship one with another, and the blood of Jesus Christ His Son cleanseth us from all sin'.

So according to Romans 8:1

> "There is therefore now no condemnation to them which are in Christ Jesus, who walk not after the flesh, but after the Spirit".

Isaiah 54:4-5,

> "Fear not; for thou shall not be ashamed (caused to Blush); neither be thou confounded; for thou shall not be put to shame; for thou shall forget the shame of thy youth, and shall not remember the reproach of thy widowhood any more. For your maker is your husband; the Lord of Host is His name, and your Redeemer the Holy One of Israel; The God of the whole earth shall He be called".

This was a promise to Israel and to the church which includes you and me; The Lord promises to remove our shame and even the memory of it. Significantly, five different words are rendered as "shame" in Isaiah 54 and are used to describe that which He will remove from us and for us. Five is the Hebrew number for 'GRACE'. God wants His people to be freed from every kind of shamefulness.

It is the will of god for us to be free from every taint of shame.

Cultural, societal, educational, or self-reformation will not free anyone from shame. Only a complete transformation from the inside can give us freedom. This must include the following: confession, repentance, forgiveness, and deliverance.

Chapter Nine

The Heart- The Hub!

The Heart is a hub. Everything we experience is processed through our hearts; the good, the bad, and the ugly. Life comes at us from all directions but everything gets channeled through our hearts. Unfortunately, our negative experiences tend to get stuck there. Eventually, they make their way out through our words and deeds but because of the delay between entry and exit, we often have a difficult time making the connection. We find that we are upset but we do not know why. We are discontent but can find no reason to feel that way, and we are resentful toward certain types of people even though they have done nothing to deserve it. We get jealous even when we know that it is foolish to dislike somebody for having something we do not have. None of these things make any sense but they are real and if left unchecked, have the potential to drive us into self-destructive and relationship-wrecking behavior or patterns.

Our Hearts being hubs extends to every conversation and dictate every relationship. Our very lives emanate from the heart. We live, parent, lead, relate, love, comfort, react, respond, instruct, manage, solve problems, and love from the heart. Our hearts impact the intensity of our communication. Our hearts have the potential to exaggerate our sensitivities and insensitivities. Every arena of life intersects with what is going on in our hearts. Everything passes through on its way to wherever it's going.

Therefore, we need to monitor our hearts closely. Life is not a level playing field and even if it were, we would still need to keep an eye on that invisible but vital part of our being:

> "Keep your heart with all diligence for out of it are the issues of life." Proverbs 4:23 (KJV)

The reality is that life is not always kind. Everyone experiences a measure of hurt and rejection, some more than others. As a result of these unavoidable realities, unpleasant things become lodged in our hearts. We have even developed language to describe this phenomenon like; "I will never trust another man", "I will never love again", "I will never give my heart to anyone", "I don't need anybody", and "I am not letting anybody in", "She broke my heart", "He wounded me". We use the following phrases to describe those whose hearts have been damaged: "She is hardhearted", "You will never get to know him", "She has walls", "He has trust issues" or "He is cold". The truth is that our earliest wounds are inflicted during childhood, at an age that prevents us from accurately processing exactly what we feel. Even worse, we do not have words to express them; all we know is that it feels bad and we do not want to feel that way ever again. If the hurt surfaces or is repeated, we begin to develop coping mechanisms as a natural response to stop the pain, and the cycle continues.

Sometimes we turn to the extreme to stop the pain because to us extreme pain calls for extreme measures. Recall how I had 'falling or fainting syndrome' which I developed whenever a father figure was around and there was no medical diagnosis for it.

Pain without a Name

A friend described how his four-year-old child experiences something called pain for the first time. They were at a party and an adult was joking around with his son about something. Suddenly, his son closed up and walked away with an expression on his face that he had never seen before and my friend knew that if this 'pain' is allowed to be logged, it will be hard to dislodge. The dilemma was how to explain to a four-year-old that the comment the adult made was just a joke. He simply said to his son, "that hurt on the inside, didn't it?" At that point, the four-year-old started crying and his father held him in his arms. This was the safest place for him to be and it was the right response, from the right person, at the right time. Those tears cleansed his little heart of the debris from the hurt he felt.

Unfortunately, for most of us, nobody was there when we received our first wound, or experienced our first dose of shame so we just carried it around with us, determined not to let it happen again. By the time we became adolescents, we all had wounded hearts. There were jabs from our friends, our parents, our teachers, our coaches, and our adversaries at school. There was no way to avoid it.

Sometimes we are born with the very thing that ends up being our source of shame. A friend shared about her terrible dentition. Her teeth were so bad that her orthodontist won an award for creating a gadget to fix her mouth. It was not just her teeth that were bad, her entire mouth was really bad. She recalled how she was abused for years because she wore braces. She was so wounded that she would refuse to smile for pictures. In every picture from fourth grade to sixth grade, she was either crying or frowning. She had no words to express the pain she felt inside when she was forced to participate in events and all the while being ridiculed and called names by other kids. Even as an adult, she still finds it difficult to smile in front of a camera.

Self-inflicted wounds

When it comes to hurt in our hearts, other people are not always to blame. The junk that gets lodged in our hearts comes from a variety of sources and as I noted earlier, sometimes we are our own worst enemy.

One example of this self-sabotaging tendency is keeping secrets. This can change hearts. The secrets can be secrets of hidden habits or secrets from our past. These secrets will cause us to build walls in our relationships. In many cases, our secrets cause us to become unjustifiably suspicious of those closest to us. The saying that 'what we usually suspect in others, we become guilty of ourselves' rings true. We carry our pains, shame, and shamefulness into our relationships. When shame is lodged in our hearts, it eventually impacts our words and behaviors.

An extreme example is an adult who suddenly remembers a chapter of abuse from his childhood, years after the incident occurred. Anyone who has been sexually abused or is married to an abused victim knows the damage done to the heart.

None of us reached adulthood without a few dents to our hearts. More importantly, our response to those things determines the condition of our hearts. We cannot control how people treat us; we cannot stop their hurtful words but we can monitor the effects on our hearts. We can also, by the special grace of God, reverse the damage and keep our hearts free from further destructive debris.

Let's talk about some of the fruits of shame which are Guilt, Anger, Greed, and Jealousy.

Guilt: I Own You

Some nouns have become verbs. Actions have been associated with some nouns so much so that they act as verbs. Guilt is such a noun. There are times when I have been forced as a result of guilt (guilted) into taking certain actions and I am sure that there have been times when we have "guilted" others into acting in our interests.

Even though Webster only defines guilt as a noun, it has been the cause of a lot of actions and reactions through the years. This is due to the 'Power of Debt' resulting from guilt. Guilt says, "I owe you" and it comes as a result of having done something we perceive to be wrong. Every wrong we do can be restated as an act of theft, as we will see in a moment. If I steal from you then I owe you. So, the message from a heart full of guilt is "I owe!" Consider the case of a man who runs off with another woman and abandons his family. Without realizing it at the time, he has stolen something from every member of his family. He stole his wife's first marriage; he has robbed her of her future, her financial security, and her reputation as a wife among other things. From his children's perspective, the man has stolen their experience of fatherhood and all that a father means to them. He has robbed them of celebrations, traditions, emotions, financial security, family moments, and so on. Initially, the man who did all this does not think in terms of what he has taken away from them. He thinks in terms of what he has gained. That changes the first time his little girl asks him why he doesn't love mom anymore and his heart is stirred. He begins to feel guilty, 'HE OWES' and debt to debtor relationship has been established.

Whenever you and I wrong another person, we create the same dynamic. The damage of personal debt can be mentally devastating. One bad decision follows another, all motivated by an excessive amount of debt. The debt created by guilt is just as devastating. Consider the man who left his family and faces a crushing debt to his kids. Most men in this situation try to "make it up" to them but the truth is that the gap has been created and can never be made up. So driven by a debt-debtor relationship, the dad compounds the problem by making a series of debt-motivated decisions. Attempts to "buy love" result in excessive materialism and a corrupted view of self-worth in the child. In an attempt to "buy some peace", many parents fail to set appropriate boundaries for kids, resulting in destructive behavior.

Hence, the IOU comes at the expense of the child, not the person carrying the debt. This is not limited to broken homes but it is also very present in marriages where the couples have decided to pursue their careers to gain financial reward, invariably and unwittingly creating an 'I OWE YOU' situation with their families. In a bid to stem the tide, permissiveness and materialism become the currency of debt payment. Once again, it is the child who loses out.

Sadly, every child who grew up in this situation knows that there is no way to make up for it. You can't replace what was taken with something else. The only way to make up for dad not being there is to do the right thing when those opportunities ever resurface. I thank God for all the second and third chances we get and even though they can never be the like the first. The best time to get it right is the first time, and due to the insidious nature of the debt, there are rarely second or third opportunities. When someone owns your money, they never seem to come to see you so usually, you must go and find them. That is the power of debt, we naturally do not want to expose ourselves to those we owe. When people are in an 'I owe you' position because of their poor choices, they look for any excuse to be absent rather than face those they owe. Even men and women who care deeply cannot overcome the sense of shame and indebtedness that their actions have brought about, and once again the offended person pays the price.

The High Cost

While having an 'I owe you' mentality can lead to bad and irrational decisions, it is the decision that you cannot make that costs you the most. Proverbs 22:7 says "the borrower is a slave to the lender". In other words, the authority belongs to those who are owed, not those who owe. This is true about moral authority as well. I have come across parents who are heartbroken because they 'perceived' that they had lost their moral authority to be guardians as they watched their children make destructive decisions. They felt that there was nothing they could do. Parents like that, find themselves in a position of debt that costs them the authority to wield the influence that every parent needs at critical times in their children's lives. More destructive decisions are made and more lives are affected as a result of an unpaid debt from guilt. Nothing less than paying the debt will relieve a guilty heart of its burden of guilt. People try to work it off, serve it off, give it off, and even try to pay it off. But no amount of good deeds, community service, charitable giving, or Sundays in the pew can relieve the guilt. It is a debt, and it must be PAID or CANCELED for a guilty heart to experience the relief that comes from healing.

Anger: You Owe Me

Guilt says, "I owe you", and anger on the other hand says, "You owe me". We generally get angry when we do not get what we want.

That is an important idea, and one thing most of us may not agree with. Still, anger is a result of not getting something we want. What we want may include something we deserve because, after all, who does not want what they deserve? A good example is when we worked hard at a job or employment and we are convinced that we deserve to be promoted, but instead, someone else got promoted. This leads us to believe that someone owes us. Just as with the family stated earlier, for the children something was taken from them. The man took off with the opportunity to have a "normal family". He stole the family unit from them. The children are convinced that someone owes them and if the father can convince the children of the reasons why he left, the debt could be transferred unwittingly over to the mother.

Show me an angry person and I will show you a hurt person. Someone owes them something, even as little as an apology. You hear phrases like "you ruined my reputation", "you stole my family", "you took the best years of my life", "you robbed me of my purity", "you owe me a raise", and "you owe me an opportunity to try", "you owe me a second chance", and "you owe me affection". The root of anger is the perception that something has been taken or stolen. Someone owes you, and now a debt to debtor relationship has been established.

The Angry Heart

It is easy to conclude that the only remedy for an angry heart is payback. After all, that is how you settle debt right? It is natural for the maxim "an eye for an eye and a tooth for a tooth" to hold sway, after all, such as the foundation of common law. People ought to pay what they owe or in the alternative given the option of a canceled debt which can also be called 'letting the person off the hook'. The irony is that the perceived debt usually cannot be paid, at least not in the same measure. How do you pay back twelve years of being absent in a child's life? It is impossible. The sad part is that people spend much of their lives waiting for debts to be paid and those debts by and large are never paid.

With the opportunity to make things right already long gone, the anger remains and in many cases, it intensifies and spreads like cancer.

The Epidemiology of anger

Anger like a virus cannot remain isolated. If anger lodges in my heart, before long, I will come to believe that everybody owes me. Therefore, we characterize certain men and women as "angry persons" because it usually seems like they are angry all the time and it shows in their demeanor.

Their wrath is not reserved for an offending party; it is not reserved for anyone and everyone. They get angry at their spouse, children, neighbors, and just about anyone who comes across their path even the government is not spared from a dose of their venom. They are equal opportunity avengers. And the closer you get, the more likely it is that you are going to get dumped on. And when it happens you ask yourself "what have I done wrong to deserve such treatment?" The answer is, that you did not let them have their way.

Then we have those who are extremely angry, nothing you do pleases them, even if you let them have their way but it ends up being not exactly the way they wanted it, you'll still get some stick. They already decided you will not get it right even before you even try. They cannot let you get it right; otherwise, they will lose their excuse to stay angry. It's sickening because anger is a disease of the heart.

Most people will say they do not have anger issues because being an angry person is not such a complimentary posture and many either deny or explain their anger away. Well, I suggest you ask those you consider to be family or close friends, listen to what they say, and most importantly listen to your feelings. Chances are that their words will stir your heart. It is when our hearts are stirred that we become most aware of who we are inside.

Also observe, that if they pause before they answer, chances are that they are afraid to tell you the truth because they feel like they are treading on very thin ice. As you listen, if you feel like a volcano slowly brewing inside, or compelled to interrupt and defend yourself, or want to just walk away, or run, that is a sure indication that there is a problem. Getting angry at your friend or family, for answering a question you asked shows that the seed of anger lodges somewhere in your heart.

Anger feeds on secrecy. Exposing it can be painful and powerful at the same time. Also, in most cases, those who love us see the anger issue, and instead of confronting us, they continue to pray that one day it will be exposed for us to see it for ourselves. Just know that this enemy in our hearts cannot withstand the light.

Sometimes, we keep it secret because we think the reason for our anger is silly and can't seem to justify being angry for so long over such a "silly act". We forget that though it may seem small and silly right now at the time of the occurrence it did not seem silly, we allow it to stay lodged in our heart and grows over the years. Anger is like cancer which usually starts at stage one in which case if arrested and treated it can be contained but when it is ignored or mistaken for some other ailment and left unattended it becomes a stage 4 cancer which is untreated and a death knell. Anger left untreated portrays us in the same light as a grumpy old man or woman.

On the other hand, you might be the kind of person who wants to tell your story every time you get a chance because you want to be understood; you enjoy the sympathy, and you have learned that people are willing to cut you some slack once they hear about all of your woes. You also know that your story helps explain your propensity to overreact, say things you later regret, punish people unfairly, and lash out at those who fall short of your expectations. In your mind, it accounts for your temper, mood swings, and your unpredictable reactions while also justifying them. But it is a built-in excuse for getting offended by anything people do not like about you. Period! It becomes a crutch because intuitively you fall back on your story every time.

Here is the truth; staying angry is like allowing people we do not like, people we no longer associate with, even people who are dead to control our lives. It was Mike Murdock that said we are angry with people and would not allow them into our houses but we carry them in our minds. It's like allowing those who have hurt us to continue to influence our current and future relationships. How long are we going to allow the people who hurt us the most, to control our lives? The reason that question can be so frustrating is that we often believe that we do not have any choice in the matter. While it is true that we cannot undo what has been done, it is equally true that we do not have to let the past control our future. We must come to terms with it and decide that we can be free. Ultimately, we must quit using our story as an excuse. The greatest gift of God to humanity is free will – the freedom of choice. We can choose whatever we want to happen to us.

The problem is that good excuses rarely 'collect dust.' We use them and use them but today we must decide to discard them. Remember, your story only explains your experience and why you behave the way you do, it does not excuse it. Until we are willing to embrace this simple but sometimes brutal truth, we will never flush the anger out of its hidden lair in our hearts. Besides, justifying our behavior by reciting our storyline only gives more power to the people who hurt us. Why should you continue to give them such leverage over your life?

Right Place, Right Time

There is an appropriate way to use your story. Not as an excuse, but as a testimony of God's love for you and His ability to free you from the past. When we allow God to have access to the part of your heart that harbors anger, something amazing will transpire. Your story will no longer explain your behavior; it will stand in stark contrast:

> "Remember ye, not the former things, neither consider the things of old. Behold, I will do a new thing; now it shall spring forth; shall ye not know it? I will make a way in the wilderness and rivers in the desert." Isaiah 43:18-19.

Perhaps you see your anger as an asset, an ally that you have learned to leverage in certain situations to get your way or to get things accomplished. You may believe that your anger makes you stronger, and you may think it makes you a better leader, parent, more effective disciplinarian, or a more successful coach. Granted, your anger probably gives you energy at times as adrenalin is pumped into you, and when harnessed and properly focused, it can be a powerful ally in certain situations but it does not make you more effective or successful and it certainly does not make you stronger. The people who are forced to interact with angry individuals often see them as weak and sometimes sick people.

Just like guilt, anger alienates us from other people. More times than we care to admit, the shrapnel of our anger pierces those closest to us; loved ones who are innocent and clueless as to what caused us to detonate in their presence. A heart filled with anger is a heart looking to be paid back. Unfortunately, in most cases, it is our unsuspecting friends and family who are made to pay the inevitable high price.

"GREED: I Owe Me

> "There is he that scatters and yet increases, and there is, that withholds more than is meet, but tends to poverty." Proverbs 11:24

Greedy individuals sincerely believe they deserve every good thing that comes their way even if greedy individuals sincerely believe they deserve every good thing that come their way even if some of those things may not be godly. They also believe that they deserve every good thing that could come their way in the future. Their mantra is, 'What's mine is mine because I have earned it and I have got a lot more on the way.' those things may not be godly. They also believe that they deserve every good thing that could come their way in the future. Their mantra is, 'What's mine is mine because I have earned it and I have got a lot more on the way.'

I know this is hard to accept but I hear people make comments like "I was just greedy, and I ate a lot of stuff" and no one considers that as an issue but when someone else would make the same comment we take it negatively. I have personally said the exact words to my children when they were younger but now that they are grown, instead, they would say to me, 'Maybe you've had too much.' My retort would always be to laugh first then say 'I don't blame you; the food was just too good.' The point is that the same set of words wreaks havoc in people's lives. Like guilt which says I owe you, anger says you owe me, and then greed says I owe me.

Consequently, it is hard to get a greedy person to part with money or stuff. Why? Because it is theirs, and they are scared of losing it. Like the angry man or woman, a greedy person usually has a story to tell and like an angry person, this story explains their propensity toward greed.

Think about this, being raised in a home with little or no financial security might explain why men or women tend to hold tight to whatever amount of money comes their way. Similarly, it is easy to understand why people who once lost everything would cling to what they have now. But greed is a different breed than the other three enemies of the heart we are discussing.

Greed always disguises itself. You may have already had a thought along the lines of; 'I don't struggle with this.' After all, you only occasionally get angry outbursts and you harbor only a few guilty secrets, and realistically we are all plagued with some level of greed in our lives. The truth is society has made it almost impossible to identify greed in our own lives. Unlike anger and guilt, greed hides behind several virtues.

Greedy people are savers, and saving is a good thing. Greedy people are often planners, and planning is good also. Greedy people want to make sure their financial future is secure, and that is a good thing as well, right? Greed is easy to hide; mostly from ourselves because the people around us know. Although it may be difficult to spot your greed in the mirror, it is not that difficult to see it in the people around us. I have heard comments from people who have a greedy uncle, father, mother, grandmother, boss, supervisor, or even client. Greedy people have this in common:

- They talk a lot about money
- They worry a lot about money.
- They are not cheerful givers.
- They are reluctant to share.
- They are sore losers.
- They quibble over insignificant sums of money.

- They always talk as if they have just enough to get by.
- They often create a culture of secrecy around them.
- They will always remind you of what they have done for you.
- They find it difficult to express gratitude.
- They are never content with what they have.
- They attempt to control people with their money.
- They possess what is called "an entitlement mentality".
- They give with strings attached.

Greed as a character trait knows no socio-economic boundaries; we have poor greedy and rich greedy individuals. Greed is not a financial issue as many may believe; it is a serious issue of the heart. Financial gains do not make people less greedy, on the contrary, financial gain or loss does not change anything, because greed emanates from the heart. Greed is a spirit and an attitude which has little bearing on what one possesses at any given time.

Greedy people are quick to make excuses and ask questions intended to make them look like they are being careful stewards when in fact they are intentionally looking for a reason not to give in the first place. If they eventually give, they make the recipient feel like they owe them something in return.

They always have strings attached to their gifts and it makes those around them feel like they are competing over stuff. It also tells them that the greedy person values stuff more than the relationship. The family member of a greedy person feels like they have to 'pay' for financial help and then they avoid bringing up financial issues around the greedy person. No wonder Jesus warned us in Luke 12:15; 'be on guard against all kinds of greed; life does not consist of an abundance of possession.' Again, of all the four heart issues above, greed is the most subtle of them all.

For a greedy person, stuff equals life. They have bought into the lie, 'my stuff is my life' and to temper with or ask for their stuff is a personal threat to them. Their possession is an extension of who they are. The truth is that we all have this kind of person described above in our families or we know someone with this heart issue.

The Driving Force

Fear is the driving force behind greed, it fuels greed and it usually manifests as fear of the unknown or what might happen. Greed is supported by an endless cast of "what ifs". What if they come asking for more of this or that? What if they scratch or break this or that? What if I do not get my fair share? What if the economy collapses?

The saddest part is people with this heart condition, fear that God either cannot or will not take care of them. Worse still, they fear that God will not take care of them in the fashion or style in which they want to be cared for.

The gap between what they suspect God might be willing to do and what they want then becomes a major source of anxiety.

So greedy people shoulder the burden to acquire and maintain everything they need to provide the sense of security they desire, or so they believe. This theory has a major problem; there is never enough. Greedy people will never have enough to satisfy their need to feel secure, every conceivable eventuality being considered. There is always another "what-if" that drives them to acquire more. Their appetite cannot be satisfied. So, they never feel they have quite enough which of course is the very thing they fear.

Consequently, greedy people rarely ever live at peace with others and never live at peace with themselves. Greed eventually strains their relationships at every level, eroding long-term relationships over things that have a shelf-life of only a few years. Except by the grace of God, the greedy people live and die in this horrible state of mind, never experiencing the joy of sharing and cheerful giving.

Jealousy: God Owes Me

As we see with each of the enemies of our hearts, they are energized by the idea that somebody owes something, guilt says, 'I owe you, anger is fueled by the notion that 'You owe me', greed is kept by the assumption that 'I owe me', and this last heart issue is no different. Jealousy says,

'God owes me. When we think about jealousy or envy, we immediately think of the things other people have that we lack; looks, skills, opportunities, health, height, inheritance, etc.

We assume our problem is with the person who possesses what we lack but let us face it, God could have fixed all of that for us. Whatever He gave your neighbor, He could have given you too. Besides, you do not want your neighbor's car, you want one like it. You do not mind the fact that God provided him with one, the problem is that you feel skipped over by God. The fact that your sister can fit comfortably into a size 3 pair of jeans is okay with you but the problem is that you can't fit. You find yourself staring at her when she is not looking thinking, 'Whoa, she looks great.' You know you should not feel this way and you try not to let it get in the way of the relationship. You may even tell your sister how good she looks, but it is always there. That niggling feeling. You are continually reminded that she has something you do not have. Most of us believe on some level that if God had taken good care of us as He has some people we know, our lives would be richer or better.

If He had made me a little "slimmer" or just a little "taller"; made me as attractive in my teens as some of my classmates; and blessed me with superior athletic ability to excel in sporting activities then I would feel better about myself so that poor or low self-esteem might not be holding me back. All the above would have changed the trajectory of my life. This list is endless. If God had made me smarter, I would have done better on my LSAT and had a shot at law school. If God had gifted me with better communication skills, I might have worked my way into a top-tier management job. If I was a more dynamic public speaker, I might have been allowed to lead a larger church, blah, blah, blah.

If you are a theist by any definition, your jealousy is an issue between you and God. What God did for one he could have done for you too, but for some reason, God chose not to.

Your problem is not with the person who has what you do not have; the problem is with God your creator. God owes you! Yet our Jealousy rarely surfaces in our interaction with God. If we are aware of it at all, we might confess it as a sin. Even then, we think of our jealousy as an issue between friends, co-workers, or neighbors. It does not register as a grudge we hold against God Himself, but that is exactly what it is. Instead, it rears its ugly head in our interaction with others.

The irony, of course, is that the people we are jealous of can do nothing to remedy the situation. Who has the power to make right the inequality between you and the people who have what you want? Can your college-degree sister or all-star brother make you a brighter person or better athlete? Can your slim best friend make you skinnier? Would it help if your neighbor gave or bought you a car just like theirs? Not really. That would make things worse.

Still, the idea of God owing you something probably strikes you the same way it did every one of us in various ways- Absurd. How could God owe me something? As Christians, we believe that I owe God everything. Perhaps that is why our jealousy is so easily misdirected, and perhaps that is why it seems impossible to conquer. If I deceive myself into believing that my problem is with others, I will never get to the root of the issue; the tension will never be resolved, never.

Only one thing serves as a remedy to my jealousy. It is when the person I envy suffers a setback of some kind. So sad indeed! In other words, the only thing the haves can do to make us, the have- nots, feel better is to lose what they have. Now none of us like to admit this, but something is satisfying about watching someone you envy lose something you wish you had. We may hate whatever it is within us that secretly rejoices in the loss of another, but it is there.

Truth be told, of the four heart invaders under consideration here, perhaps jealousy betrays the true condition of our heart more than any other. I can justify my efforts to conceal my past; I can make a convincing case for my anger, and my greed is easy to camouflage behind the virtues of stewardship and prudence. But how do you justify those incriminating feelings or loss of satisfaction when someone you know (and even love) suffers a setback or loss of some kind? Before you know it, with no conscious effort on your part, there it is that despicable feeling of satisfaction. And where did it come from? Straight from the heart.

They are not my problem!

The reason the people I envy cannot do anything to remedy my feelings is that they are not my problem. Their losses, setbacks, failures, and extra poundage only temporarily alleviate and do not eradicate my pain, because if it is not them, it will be someone else.

There will always be richer, better placed or positioned, more talented, better connected, or luckier people than me and you. Until I find a way to deal with my jealous heart, I will be unable to follow the most basic of all Christian tenets–*love your neighbor.*

If jealousy rages unchecked, no relationship I have will be safe. Period! Not one! No environment will escape the effect of jealousy. Envy is a powerful force that can wreak irreparable damage upon any relationship or organization. The irony and tragedy are that the remedy cannot be found by balancing the scales or even by tipping them in the other person's favor. The fact is that somebody's upset with God, and in most cases, the person does not even know it.

As they always say, seeing the problem is half of the solution. Yeah, the easy half. Now the question is what do we do with these four heart issues: guilt, anger, greed, and jealousy, or worse yet, about them? Do we ignore the enemies attacking our hearts as so many of us do with our cholesterol and high blood pressure? Or do we search for a cure?

According to John Welwood, 'the most powerful agent of growth and transformation is something much more basic than any technique: a change of heart.'

Chapter Ten

No Pain no Gain

It is like when you visit a doctor's clinic and after a series of tests, he tells you that you have a heart condition. He tells you that on a scale of 1-10, the condition of your heart is 7, with 10 being the worst, and the doctor gives you a three-day-a-week exercise regime. One would expect that the doctor will recommend something more drastic than the exercise but the doctor knows that by exercising, the heart muscles get strengthened just like any muscle you exhaust, it is exercising that resets it. The sweat and the soreness are all part of the treatment, and although it may not feel good at the time, it is the right road to recovery.

Again, just as with our physical hearts, we try to avoid the pain of a healthy heart with God by giving Him all kinds of reasons. In churches all over the world, people stand together and sing, "Change my heart oh God, make it ever new; change my heart oh God, let me be like you". I wish it were that easy. Sometimes with prayers, maybe. It sure requires effort, sometimes it requires pain, and there is always some discomfort involved.

A changed heart is a result of forming some new habits; some exercise for the heart. For that reason, most of us would rather sing about it than do the hard work. Just like with prayers, we read books on prayers, we talk about prayers, we teach about prayers, we sing about prayers, and we do all other things but pray. Sadly, we cannot expect to break a bad habit overnight. It takes a new habit to break an old habit. We can pray every day for a generous heart, but until we start exercising our hearts in that direction, nothing is going to change.

Like the saying; 'Old habits die hard', guilt, anger, greed, and jealousy are all habit-forming phenomena and like any habit that goes unchecked, over time they come to define us. This disorder becomes such a big part of us that we no longer see them as issues to be resolved. Instead, we dismiss these destructive habits as characteristics hard-wired into our personality; 'That is just the way I am.' The men in my family are famous for their tempers, what can I say? "I am a saver". It's just like me saying that I just enjoy eating as an excuse for a lack of self-control with food. In other words, I was simply born with a greater propensity for culinary delectation than the average person. Another one is me believing the lie that being fat is part of who I am, and that my size has nothing to do with habits that need to be changed. We tend to laugh off our bad habits as 'personality traits,' but that does not change the truth; they are habits and destructive habits need to be broken.

We pray for change while we make excuses for the things that we need to change. We want to wake up one morning with a generous spirit, a guilt-free spirit, and an anger-free spirit. But when the time comes to do the heavy lifting, doing those habit-breaking exercises necessary to bring about change, something in us resists: "if God wants to change me overnight, fine, but if you are asking me to work at it, then maybe you are trying to make me somebody that I am not, right?

Thank God we have solutions to the four heart conditions I described, four specific spiritual exercises that if we will make them a habit, will effectively neutralize the enemies of our heart.

Like physical exercise, implementing this regime is often a matter of sheer discipline, an act of the will so to say, a feeling-defying act of the will. And like physical exercise, these internal "stretches" are always profitable, even when they are not especially enjoyable.

The Longer one has been living with guilt, hanging on to anger, clinging to stuff, or comparing oneself to others, the harder it will be to exercise these four virtues. The longer I neglected my heart, the harder it became to get it back into shape. But in the end, every exercise will be worth the effort.

It's hard to find a physically fit person that regrets the effort of hard work. The same applies to good habits, but we all know people who are paying a price for bad habits they never worked on.

Some people consistently practice the four habits we are about to discuss. There is just something about their lives that shows you the healthy condition of their hearts. It is so obvious because they are happy, genuinely happy, and a joy to be around.

Joyful/Happiness

Being joyful, happy, and staying that way is a quest we all enter this world with. But most of us think we can squeeze it out of something or someone else, and that never works, especially for the person being squeezed.

None of us is born with them, they are learned behaviors. Joyful people seem to do them instinctively. And we tend to think, he or she is always gracious, kind, and humble, but that is rarely the story.

Over time these habits have helped to shape the individual's character and relationship patterns, often because they grew up in an environment where these habits were taught and modeled. We are tempted to think that joyfulness or happiness is simply a matter of disposition or the product of circumstance, but that is not the truth, we know people who are in less than enviable circumstances who are genuinely happy people to be around.

On the other hand, we know people with more stuff than they know what to do with, who are never content.

Why? I am glad you asked. It's because joy and happiness are not synonymous with wealth, nor are they synonymous with beauty, marriage, singleness, or any other external circumstance or relational status.

We know wealth works against joy or happiness. Typically, the more a person has, the less generous they become. The more a person has, the more anxiety they experience. Also, the more they become insatiable; they always find someone to compete with. The good news is that even the wealthy can effect changes to their heart habits. Joyfulness or happiness is no respecter of persons but it is the overflow of a healthy heart.

Chapter Eleven

Habit #1- Confronting Guilt

Secrets lose their power when exposed to light. The light that exposes our secrets and frees the heart from the oppressive nature of guilt is *confession*. This is not the Webster's definition of confession, which defines it as a simple admission of culpability in a particular incident': 'Yes Judge, that light was red,' this kind of confession eases our conscience temporarily but does nothing to expose the deeper secrets that keep our hearts in turmoil.

Worse still, this kind of confession can fuel destructive behavior rather than curb it, leading to more secrets and greater guilt. It is similar to the loophole that can be noticed in 1 John 1:9 which says, "If we confess our sins, He is faithful and just to forgive us our sins and cleanse us from all unrighteousness." Means 'I mess up, I admit. God forgives me, I move on.' A friend shared how every night he would go through a monologue detailing all his sins to God, remembering all the sins he committed that day.

He mentioned them all, short or long, all he said wrong, done wrong, and simply add whatever he had overlooked before going to sleep, to make sure that at least his sin bucket was empty! But at the back of his mind, he knew he would probably fill the bucket up again the very next day, in fact, most likely with the same sins.

Then he noticed a dangerous trend. When he was tempted to sin, he would reason to himself, "Hey! I know this is wrong but doing it is ok if I confess it, and God will forgive me". Before long, his confession habit began to support his sin habit.

We have our loopholes and we use the scriptures to rubber-stamp our choices and make them mean exactly what we want them to mean. This was a routine during my high school days at St. Dominic School, a Catholic school, but my loophole was confessing to a Priest. The truth is that none of this practice was done as a step towards any heart transformation or change.

Confession was just about guilt relief–a bandage covering something deeper. We were made to go to confession three times every week; Monday, Wednesday, and Friday. Each of us had our version of the confession game. None of us was interested in changing anything, but we sure felt better about ourselves.

The cloud lifts and the slates are clean. Now that we have gotten God off our case, surely now God will be on our side. Realistically, none of us will side with someone who treats us this way. Imagine a scenario where you had

Habit #1- Confronting Guilt

a brother who continually stole from you, embarrassed you publicly, and talked badly about you behind your back but once a week he would come to you and say how sorry he was. No sooner than his apology, did he turn around and do the same thing again. The cycle was then set: do wrong, ask for forgiveness, and get back to it. Even if you can forgive each time, eventually there will be no relationship because you will feel used and even insulted. You will then begin to question the sincerity of his apology.

Let's face it; our approach to confession is an insult to God, our Heavenly father. We would certainly not dream of staying in such a relationship with anyone who treated us that way. Thank God that His love for us is unconditional, otherwise, we would all be in serious trouble.

So, what went wrong, why the endless circle? Why have we allowed confession to become a tool that facilitates and empowers our sin rather than ending it all together? We play the confession game because somewhere along the way we have been taught that the purpose of confession was 'conscience relief'. Some even think confession makes God feel better about our sins and confession puts everything back to the way it was. Really? How can confession to God about what I have done to someone else make everything right? How does that restore anything? What about the person I wronged? Not only does it not make sense, but it also does not work.

Confession is only an admission of wrongdoing and that is where it ends. To change one's habits goes beyond mere confession. This pseudo-confession does not remove our guilt. Like Tylenol, our quick confession prayers take the edge off our pain, but they do not heal the disease because they are caused by sin. Therefore, we find ourselves confessing and then repeating the sins of our past, so the guilt is still there.

Confession: in the Bible

Webster's definition of confession is 'to admit to or acknowledge something'. But in the bible, confession is associated with ***change.*** Confession is just one step in the sequence of steps that lead the guilty out of darkness and into the light. It is simply the beginning of a process that ultimately leads to a change in lifestyle or behavior.

The word 'penance' is associated with change or repentance. Repentance is often pictured as a person who is walking in one direction and turning in the opposite direction. In the scriptures, confession is connected with restitution, repentance, and restoration.

In the Old Testament, confession was always public and was associated with restitution (Numbers 5: 6-7). In fact, for the Jew, this was not about feeling better about themselves; it was about making things right with the one you sinned against. **It was not enough to be sorry, you had to pay back with interest.**

God was interested in change and having to go public with your sin and make restitution certainly motivates people to change. Recall that John the Baptist called people to repentance as well as the confession of sins (Mark 1: 4-5). This was certainly not a private confession, it was a public confession made in connection with public repentance. His audience was going public intending to live a different kind of life. They were not confessing just to silence their conscience; they were ready to leave their sins behind and head in a different direction.

Confession was not simply a means to feeling better about their sins; it was a public step toward abandoning sin altogether.

In the New Testament, we find the infamous tax collector Zacchaeus following this Old Testament model of confession but instead of the required one-fifth that God instituted in the law, Zacchaeus gave back four times what he had taken illegally. Note that Zacchaeus is not the cute short man depicted in our childhood Sunday school classes. He was a wicked man considered a traitor to his nation. He wronged many of his fellow Jews, leaving a trail of wreckage in his wake. But when Jesus invited Himself over to Zacchaeus's house that fateful day, the little tax collector was changed forever. He found in Jesus the hope and forgiveness he had since given up on. Zacchaeus knew instinctively that it was not enough to confess his sin to Jesus. That was only the first step: 'Look, Lord! Here and now, I give half of my possessions to the poor, and if I have cheated anybody out of anything, I will pay back four times the amount.' (Luke 19:8). Jesus did not stop him from saying well Zacchaeus, 'Oh no, you are forgiven! It is enough that you confessed your sins to me; there is no need to make a public spectacle of yourself. Instead, Jesus said in effect, 'Now I know for sure that salvation has come to this house. Your public admission is evidence of a changed heart.' Zacchaeus did not just admit to his sins of the past, but he also took responsibility for them. He confessed in the truest sense of the term.

Over and over the Bible speaks of confession, not in terms of conscience relief but terms of a visible life change. Never is confession offered as a substitute for repentance. It is but a step toward repentance. "And the prayer offered in faith will make the sick person well; the Lord will raise them. If they have sinned, they will be forgiven. Therefore, confess your sins to each other and pray for each other so that you may be healed" (James 5:15-16).

James calls for confession to one another as part of our restoration. James seems to indicate that illness is sometimes caused by hidden sin. Regardless of your thoughts on that point, do not miss the implication of James' words: Because hidden sin may be the cause of visible illness, the smartest thing to do is confess, not only to God but to other people.

In other words, bring your secrets into the light. According to this passage, confession precedes physical and spiritual restoration. Again, there is nothing here about relieving your conscience or feeling better about yourself, or wiping the slate clean with God. Confession is the first step toward change.

Keep First Things First

No doubt this is what Jesus had in mind when He shocked His listeners with this statement, "Therefore if you are offering your gift at the altar and there remember that your brother or sister has something against you, leave your gift there in front of the altar, first go and reconcile with them; then come and offer your gift". (Matthew 5:23-24).

We can just imagine what Jesus' audience will be thinking, "Now Jesus, you mean after waiting in line in the temple for half a day with an acceptable sacrifice, I am supposed to tie up my lamb or hand my pigeon off to someone else, just to go make peace with someone mad at me?" Well, this was certainly a new wrinkle on the law. Not only was it new but it was also inconvenient. Besides, wasn't our relationship with God supposed to be our ultimate priority? Isn't God more interested in our getting right with him than in us getting things right with our next-door neighbor? Are we not supposed to put God first? Certainly, we should be concerned about a strained relationship but surely it could wait until after Church.

No, Jesus in effect said our relationship with God hinges on our relationship with other people, the two are inseparable. This implies that our ability to worship God sincerely and fellowship with Him unashamedly is contingent upon the status of our relationships with others, including those we have offended.

The truth is we cannot resolve our differences with God if we are unwilling to resolve our differences with others around us. We cannot be in fellowship with the father and out of fellowship with other people, the two go together.

Confessing secretly to God or a priest is no substitute for confessing openly to someone we wronged. God values relationships and considers restoration a priority. Often, that requires confession, not just to God, but to the offended party. Part of walking with God is making that call we dread making, setting up that appointment we know would be incredibly awkward, writing that letter that you should have written long ago. It means humbling yourself, owning up to your part of the problem, and doing everything within your power to make those relationships right. And when you swallow your pride and take that extra step, something remarkable happens. Guilt loses its foothold over your heart and the power of sin is broken in your life.

Open confession has the power to break the cycle of sin. That is the purpose of confession, and like medicinal remedies, it works when we apply the principle properly. If we start confessing our sins to each other, chances are that we are not going back and committing those same sins again. Maybe that is the reason we would rather just confess our sins to God; it gives us a cop-out. We can be repeat offenders without embarrassing ourselves. Hence, we confess secretly, and in many cases, we know we are going to repeat the same sin.

For example, if I confess to my sales manager that I inflated the sales numbers last quarter, assuming I keep my job, the odds are that I would not inflate the numbers again, right? Not if it means I must confess the same infraction a second time.

Also, if I muster the courage to confess to a friend, that I told someone else something they had told me in confidence, chances are that I will never do that again, not if it means having to confess it again.

Guilty people statistically are repeat offenders and if we are carrying or keeping a secret; if we are trying to ease our conscience by only telling God how sorry we are, we are setting ourselves up to repeat the past. However, the way God designed confession to be applied breaks the cycle of sin and guilt. Again, that is just the beginning.

The reason we still feel guilty about things in our past is that they are still unresolved. Telling God alone, we are sorry does not resolve our guilt because God was not the only offended party.

Talking to God is not just enough; our burden of guilt will not be lifted until we confess to the offended party. Then and only then can we live out in the open. Only then will we be free from the secrets that have formed walls between us and the people we love most. However, I must caution that it requires wisdom to do this the right way. We must ensure that our confession to the offended individual does not further aggravate the issue.

Do not Misplace or Abuse Grace

Some might argue and say this about forgiveness; 'God has forgiven all our sins, why do I still need to dredge up a bunch of stuff from the past when it has all been paid for at the cross? Besides, I was not a Christian when I did some of those wrongs.'

Well, the Bible cannot contradict itself. I used those same arguments for a long time, but when all the theological gymnastics were finished my guilt remained. Why? Because God was not the only offended party. Remember, the same Bible that talks about forgiveness also teaches the principle of restitution.

Forgiveness doesn't erase our need to take responsibility for what we have done wrong. Forgiveness should drive our confession. I believe part of the confusion in this area stems from a misapplication of the doctrine of grace. When we became Christians, we came face to face with the unconditional, undeserved, unmerited grace of God. It is quite overwhelming to realize that there was nothing we could do to earn our forgiveness or our salvation. It was a gift, period! Nothing we did had any merit. Our good deeds did not, and could not, earn our good standing with God.

But that is not the case with our relationships with others. God has forgiven us, but those we have wronged and angered may not have. They may very well be held hostage to bitterness and anger over what was done to them. We must be kidding ourselves if we think that everyone we have wronged has simply forgiven us and gone on with their lives. Sure, that is what they ought to do, but if people always did what they "ought to do", forgiveness would not be an issue for any of us in the first place, right? Worse still, we have convinced ourselves that we are not responsible for making restitution:

> "Therefore if you are presenting your offering at the altar, and there remember that your brother has something against you. Leave your offering there before the altar and go; first, be reconciled to your brother and then come and present your offering." Matthew 5:23-24 (NAS)

The Grace that was showered on us at the point of salvation did not provide us with an escape hatch from our responsibilities to others. On the contrary, that very grace should compel us to make restitution to those we have wronged. Christ paid a debt he did not owe and one we could not pay! That kind of love should motivate us to pay those debts we 'can' pay to those we owe.

The good news is, that the penalty for our sins, as far as heaven and hell are concerned, has been dealt with once and for all. The *consequences* of our sins are a different matter altogether. We are avoiding one of the fundamental clear teachings of the Bible if we use our forgiveness as an excuse to avoid the pain and embarrassment of reconciling with others.

Indeed, we can never repay God for all He has done for us, but we may certainly be able to repay our fellow men for what we have done to them. Doing so is the only way to free ourselves and our hearts from the poison of guilt once and for all.

To understand the power of confession, just put yourself on the receiving end. Think for a moment, whose apology do we most desire and least expect? Imagine how we would feel if we got a surprise visit from such a person. How would we feel if that individual walked in and took full responsibility for what they did? Imagine what might transpire in our hearts if, with sincere humility, that person offered to do anything within their power to make restitution for what had been taken from us. I believe we would never be the same. It would be almost impossible to resist the changes that would begin to take place in our hearts. That is the power of confession. Not only does it have the potential to free us from our guilt, but it may also be the path to forgiveness for those we have hurt. Indeed, our words may bring healing to a wounded soul.

Habit #1- Confronting Guilt

Perhaps the greatest consequence, of our unwillingness to own up to our responsibilities, is that it fuels the fire of bitterness and anger in someone else's life. For many of us who have been hurt and whose souls are filled with self-destructive fury, a simple confession could set us free. All such an individual needs to do to be released from the eroding forces of bitterness is to go to the offended party and make it right; to say that they know they could never repay the offended fully or make it go away, but they want the offended party to know that they are responsible and are sincerely sorry, and they are willing to do whatever it takes to make up to the offender.

For someone reading this, you hold the last piece of a puzzle that a man or woman has been attempting to complete for a long time. Owning up to "your" responsibility may be the thing that equips this man or woman to move on with life. Simply confessing to God alone does not accomplish that. Confessing to God will not fully set our hearts free from the guilt that is slowly eating away at our characters and conscience.

God's forgiveness doesn't exempt us from the responsibility of confession and restitution. On the contrary, God's forgiveness is the very reason to confess and reconcile with the other party. God paid a high price to reconcile us back to Him and now God is calling on us to pay the price to reconcile with each other.

Guilt Trip

Sometimes now or later, in our life's journey on this side of heaven, God is going to call on us all to turn around and take responsibility for our past. Unresolved relationships, debts that have been neglected, apologies never made; these are things God will eventually lead us to own and resolve.

How does God do this? Through that nagging, undeniable, irritating sense of guilt that follows us around like a bad cold. We cannot confess it away, fast it away or pray it away. *Understanding God's "Descriptive and Permissive Will" is crucial to being free.*

Sure, it is painful. Yes, it can be inconvenient, embarrassing, and humiliating at times. Think about it this way, our Lord and Savior suffered a painful, inconvenient, and humiliating death on a Roman cross for the sake of our past and future sins; they were not even His own.

Jesus took responsibility for the sins of the whole world and died so that all men and women could be reconciled to the father. Think about it, in the shadow of the cross all our excuses, all our griping, our entire rationalizations amount to nothing. We have no excuse for Jesus' death was for our good, and His command regarding confession and reconciliation is for our good also. Jesus wants us to be completely free from sin's enslavement. Confession enables us to come out from the shadow of sin and into the light where all things are made new!

Conscious Confession versus Unconscious Holiness

A habit of conscious confession will invariably lead to a life of unconscious Holiness. It must become a habit in our lives.

I had to learn this the hard way. Once I moved beyond my self-deception, I got busy and cleaned the slate, not with God, but with other people I wronged, hurt, or offended. Since then, confession has become a habit.

We must choose between self-respect and public respect. I believe self-respect is more important. Why pollute my heart with guilt to protect a reputation I may not have anyway? Remember, the purpose of confession is not to relieve your conscience; it is to effect change and reconciliation.

Simply put, just leverage this powerful tool in the way it was intended. Go public with your sin and purge your heart of guilt that is eroding your confidence and faith. It is hard to imagine that breaking a deliberate habit can be done without going public. A good example is an AA (Alcoholic Anonymous). The folks are told that going public with a habit is the first and possibly the most important step in recovery.

Confession breaks the death grip of guilt and sets us free to embrace the future God has for us without dragging around the dead bones of the past.

The consequence of confession is far less severe than the consequence of concealment. Secrets are like a buried splinter: The best thing to do is to get them out; otherwise, the wound will get infected. Healing cannot begin until the splinter is out and until you and I confess. Sure, it hurts, but guess what? Over time, ignoring the splinter causes you deeper pain and more complications. Confession is a habit worth forming.

Chapter Twelve

Habit #2- Confronting Anger

I believe of the four enemies vying for control of our hearts, anger is the most obvious and perhaps the most dangerous. Anger when unleashed with unbridled intensity, leaves a trail of destruction in its wake.

But behind all the huffing, puffing, ranting, raving, brewing, and stewing are the most basic tenets of human experience: we just cannot get our way! The angry person approaches life, love, and relationships like a person who's being owed and is looking for ways to be paid back! Anger says, 'You owe me and it often discriminates about who is going to be made to pay. Suffice it to say that the only remedy to anger is forgiveness. Whereas guilty people need to get in the habit of confessing, angry people need to develop the habit of forgiving, but it is not easy. We all have tried to forgive, and nothing changed.

There is as much confusion over what it means to forgive, so much so that many of us feel like we are stuck.

We can be grouped into three categories: The first group believes they ought to forgive but cannot seem to muster the courage to do it; The second group feels they would be letting the offender off the hook, and that does not seem right; and the third group claims to have gone through the motions of forgiveness, but those old feelings and memories keep coming back, leaving them to wonder if they had ever really forgiven the offender at all.

Another dilemma people face is the requirement to forgive and forget. When someone tries to forgive the offender but each time the thought of what transpired comes to mind, bitterness seems to begin to resurface. The solution to this puzzle is the fact that forgiving someone and forgetting are two different issues entirely. In practical terms, there are mutually exclusive! You can forgive someone but remember what they did not because you want to seek revenge but because you have to be wiser in your relationship with such a person.

The following are legitimate questions that beg for honest answers: 'How do you forgive someone? How do you know if you have forgiven them? What if the other person is a repeat offender? What if you do not know how to get in touch with the offending party? What if you cannot stomach the idea of getting in touch with the offender in the first place? What if the offender is no longer alive?

An Unrealistic Request

Even though Christ has given us the ultimate example of sacrificial love and forgiveness, the question of what to do with our anger continues to be an issue for all Christ-followers. The Apostle Paul in Ephesians 4:31 told the Ephesian Church "Get rid of all bitterness, rage, and anger, brawling, and slander, along with every form of malice."

We are commanded to get rid of anger. This didn't even make much sense to me initially because of the struggle of what to do with my emotions? The Greek term translated here as "get rid of" means "to remove; to separate yourself from."

This is the picture I have in mind: Have you ever unintentionally walked through a spider's web? You are be-bopping along, humming a tune then you walk straight into arachnophobia. Well, in Africa, this was quite common. What do you do? I can tell you what I would do. I frantically begin to pull at anything and everything that remotely feels like a spider web. Off my face, out of my hair. Off my clothes! Now that is the idea that "get rid" represents. Get it off and get it off quick! Again, Paul says "ALL". Paul helps us by listing every relational wedge – bitterness, rage, anger, brawling, and malice. The definition of Malice is "General ill will towards another person". That means whatever negative emotions you and I are harboring, regardless of who we are harboring it against, need getting rid of!

One may argue that Paul lived two thousand years ago and has no idea about what is going on in our lives today. It is similar to a total stranger walking up to you and demanding that you get rid of all your bitterness towards your ex-husband or ex-wife or whoever is driving you nuts. Well, my guess is the G-rated version would simply be "mind your own business!" Besides, the stranger might not know the entire story! The truth is that we may have a really convincing story because we have the right to be mad and stay mad! In the end, the stranger might conclude that you did not deserve the treatment you got and that the offender does not deserve to get away with it.

Apostle Paul is Credible!

The Scripture told us that Paul dictated those words from his cell in a Roman prison. Arrested unjustly and extradited to Rome, he had been awaiting trial for more than a year when those words were written. To make matters worse, the political climate in Rome was not favorable to Believers at all. This "Way or Cult" as it was termed was viewed with great suspicion by the population as well as the leadership.

Despite these less-than-ideal circumstances, Paul instructs believers to "rid" themselves of all traces of bitterness and anger. Also, Paul did not give terms or conditions for his words. No exceptions were given.

Habit #2- Confronting Anger

I believe Paul knew with all certainty that there is a sure way to "rid" ourselves of our bitterness and anger. Carrying around the list Paul spoke about can make life a big struggle and quite complicated. I'm sure you'd agree with me that Life is hard enough as it is. So why make it harder? I know it does not sound realistic, you may say after all your anger, and bitterness is simply a response to the people around you. You are just reacting and it is not your fault and besides the fact that it is not your fault, there is nothing you can do about it. And so, every day you have this rage going on inside of you. The question is, how can we possibly get rid of our anger when our anger is simply a justified response to stuff done to us that we have no control over?

So, we begin to get defensive with claims like 'I am the victim of hurt, rejection, criticism, betrayal, and many more wrongs.' All these and so much more leave us feeling like victims. Then we lash out. Who can truly blame us? Victims are powerless. Victims have no control over their lives. Victims are at the mercy of others, and victims can only react! Victims are held prisoner by circumstances generally beyond their control! It is these feelings of victimization that fuel our justifications and excuses.

Take note, a victim will always, always have an excuse. A victim can write off just about any kind of behavior. With what he or she had to endure, they would feel that we should expect these types of attitudes from them. The victim mentality creates an unassailable wall of excuses and rationalizations. In time we come to believe the lie: "It is ok to behave the way you do. You sure have no choice. For you, this behavior is perfectly acceptable. You are under no obligation to change, and you have every right to be the way you are". In the end, we have no incentive whatsoever to change.

The abnormal becomes normal to us; it becomes an auto default setting. We end up staying in the same spot because change is work! Victims do not want to be proactive about changing, they want to be proactive about making sure that the person who hurt them *pays*. Then we expend our energy telling our sad stories repeatedly rather than taking responsibility for our behavior. Thereby opening the door of our hearts and welcoming the Trojan horse of bitterness as a monument, a constant reminder of a debt someone has not yet paid, somebody owes us. In time, everybody begins to owe us. So, when we read, "get rid of all bitterness, rage and anger, brawling, and slander, along with every form of malice", we think "there is no way". It's out of our control we are only responding to the people and world around us. "I cannot get rid of that stuff". Well, you are right. You can't, not at your current capacity at least.

Divine Formula

Chemistry, physics, and statistics are full of "formulas". So, what did Paul know that we do not know on this subject matter? What formula did he have to be able to speak with such authority to people whose circumstances he was unfamiliar with?

Ephesians 4:31-32 "Be kind and compassionate to one another, forgiving each other..." Paul is saying, in contrast to bitterness and brawling, we extend "kindness and compassion" to those who have wronged us, and then we *forgive*. The sentence structure of the scripture simply implies that *forgiveness* is, how we are to do away or *rid* ourselves of bitterness, rage, and anger. That forgiveness is what enables us to be kind and compassionate to people who have given us either kindness or compassion.

Now, if Apostle Paul had stopped there, we could retreat to our well-rehearsed excuses about how badly we have been treated and how unfair life has been, because of the wrong done to us. If he had put a period at the end of 'other', we could no doubt argue convincingly that the people, who wronged or fueled our anger and bitterness do not deserve to be forgiven.

Most of them do not even consider themselves in need of any forgiveness because they are not even aware that they have done anything wrong. Even when they are, some still believe they do not need our forgiveness and this is the part that hurts the most.

Praise God, Paul did not stop there; He frames the concept of forgiveness in a way that should cause all of us to pause and reconsider this ancient concept. Ephesian 4:32, "Be kind and compassionate to one another, forgiving each other, *just as in Christ, God forgave you!*" So incredible and profound! In the application and principle, the kindness and forgiveness Paul refer to are fueled by an attitude of forgiveness, but not just any forgiveness. This forgiveness must mirror the kind God extended towards us in Christ Jesus. This, I must confess, carries more weight and significance than we can ever understand.

"Just as" is exactly what gave Apostle Paul the confidence to write about this standard of behavior that most would consider unrealistic.

Even, more importantly, the phrase "Just as" is the key to allowing God to rid our hearts of bitterness and resentment that have the potential to plant their destructive tentacles into every important relationship we have. "Just as" clearly redefines and upgrades the meaning of "forgiveness".

You! Are the Benefactors

How do we set limits? Fortunately for you and me, Jesus tackled the issue of forgiveness head-on during His earthly ministry. Interestingly, it was confusion over this issue of resolving relational conflicts that allowed Jesus to redefine forgiveness for us all! Praise God for that.

Matthew 18:21-25, here Apostle Peter, as a disciple of Jesus understood his responsibility to forgive, but he was not sure how far to take it. In other words, what is the acceptable limit? What do you do about the person

Habit #2- Confronting Anger

who hurts you repeatedly? So, Peter pulled Jesus aside and asked sincerely. "How often shall my brother sin against me and I forgive him? Up to seven times?" In other words, when is enough, enough? How many times do I need to forgive? When is it all right not to forgive? Again, Peter was very sincere in his question. He wanted to do the right thing and expected that at least there must be a limit. Where is justice in a system where forgiveness is offered at every turn? Just like us, Peter gave it his best shot, at what he considered to be generous enough. What about seven times Jesus? (The number 7 in the Bible is the number of completion).

Peter was on the right track here and was starting to catch on. No doubt, there was a time in Peter's hard-knocked life when Peter would have suggested, "two times" or possibly one time. But Peter had been with Jesus and had been listening. Peter knew that Jesus' perspective on things was quite different from that of the religious teachings of his days. He wanted to test that by asking how often I shall forgive. Peter revealed his misunderstanding of the nature of forgiveness that Jesus is talking about. Like most of us, Peter assumed that "Forgiveness is for the benefit of the offender". That's not true and will never be.

Like most of us, Peter was willing to stretch a bit, to be the "nice man or woman" he was willing to go as many as seven times with the same person over the same issue. But after that or some other predetermined point–no more. After all, forgiveness has its limit and everybody knows that. I can just imagine Jesus looking straight at Peter with a graceful smile and one hand on Peter's shoulder, saying "I tell you, not seven times, but seventy times seven" Predictably, before Peter could respond, Jesus offered one of His most intriguing parables:

> "Therefore, the kingdom of heaven is like a king who wanted to settle accounts with his servants. As he began the settlement, a man who owed him ten thousand bags of gold was brought to him. Since he was not to pay, the master ordered that he and his wife and his children and all that he had be sold to repay the debt. At this, the servant fell to his knees before him. "Be patient with me", he begged, "and I will pay back everything". The servant's master took pity on him, canceled the debt, and let him go". Matthew 18:23-27.

The thing that makes this parable so helpful is that Jesus talks about the emotionally charged topic of forgiveness in a way that everybody can understand. He takes the mystery out of it.

Simply put, forgiveness is the decision to cancel a debt. This is so simple, so practical, but so easily missed! Yes, you read that right, missed.

Habit #2- Confronting Anger

Remember, whenever someone hurts you, there is a sense in they have taken something from you, and debt is incurred. For example, If somebody gossips about you, it amounts to that person stealing your good reputation. When an employer fires a worker unjustly, the employer robs the worker of his or her financial security. If a man is unfaithful to his wife, he robs her of emotional security and perhaps much more. If the wife is unfaithful to her husband, she is robbing him of his self-worth.

Wherever it is hurt, there is a theft. There is an imbalance because somebody owes someone. Therefore, we hear comments like "I am going to get even with her". To achieve justice, a transaction must take place that transfers something back to the victim. It could be an apology, a favor, money, or some other form of restitution but the tension will remain until the debt is settled.

Just like in the parable, the master was going to settle his debt with the servant by selling the servant's wife, his children, and all his possessions, something he had every right to do under the ancient law. The servant, on the other hand, did the only thing he could; He pleaded for mercy, then he did something rather absurd; he promised to pay his debt. Ten thousand talents were an enormous amount of money, more money than the servant would make in a lifetime. His debt was beyond his ability to repay. Fortunately for him; his master was a merciful man. The master took pity on his servant and canceled his debt.

He decided to forego his right to be paid back, and that is the essence of forgiveness: a decision to cancel a debt. It would have been nice if Jesus ended the parable there, but Jesus continued: "But when that servant went out, he found one of his fellow servants who owed him a hundred silver coins. He grabbed him and began to choke him. "Pay back what you owe me" he demanded, His fellow servant fell to his knees and begged him, "be patient with me, and I will pay it back" (Matthew 18:28-29).

Here the roles were reversed, we find the forgiven servant in the position of his master, in a place of power. His fellow servant owed him a hundred silver coins, a small amount that no doubt his fellow servant could have come up with given a bit of time, and we would expect this man whose massive debt had just been forgiven to extend the same grace to his fellow servant. Instead, he had the man thrown into prison until he could pay the debt. He chose to hold this unfortunate fellow to the original agreement. He had him thrown in prison until he or a family member could raise the money to pay the debt in full.

As we all know, things have a way of coming full circle. The parable continued; "when the other servants saw what had happened, they were outraged and went and told their master everything that had happened, then the master called the servant in, "You wicked servant", he said, "I canceled all that debt of yours". (Verse 31-32). Here is the Biblical/scriptural definition of forgiveness; "Canceled debt". The master continued; "I canceled all that debt of yours because you begged me to, shouldn't you have had mercy on your fellow servant just as I had on you?" (Verse 32-33).

So, I am quite sure everyone listening to the parable nodded vigorously and thought "Gee! Come on bro! Of course, he should have had mercy on his fellow servant". Again, the word "Mercy" was intentionally used by Jesus in this parable (Mercy: Not giving me what I deserve). The parable continues; 'in anger, his master turned him over to the jailer... until he should pay back all he owed (verse 34). And rightly so! Anybody that is ungrateful deserves to pay his debt. This was not extraordinary punishment; this was simply a matter of holding the servant to his end of the original arrangement. He owed and he would have to pay.

But in the next statement, Jesus said something no one expected, if Peter was still wondering what any of this had to do with his original question, he was about to get an awakening! A painfully clear one. "This is how my heavenly Father will treat each of you unless you forgive your brother or sister from your "heart"! Whoa! If the meaning of the parable was not clear at the beginning, it became crystal clear at this point.

The king in the parable represents God, and the servant who had his debts forgiven represents everybody who has his or her sin canceled by God and wouldn't know it. The second servant is anyone who we are holding something against because of something they had done to us. These are the people who have offended us, hurt us, betrayed us, embarrassed us, abandoned us, rejected us, slandered us, or lied against us. In other words, the people who owe us are the people we have a legitimate case against, and Jesus is saying emphatically: cancel their debt, forgive them, or else. What a terrible thing to tell someone who has been taken advantage of! I know what you are thinking, "Give me a break, I have already been hurt once", or "can't you see that I am the victim here". Now you are telling me that if I do not grant forgiveness to this person who has done such a horrible thing to me, then God is coming after me too?

Divine Perspective

Honestly, I am not too sure what is meant by "Father will treat each of you", but clearly, this was meant as a stern warning to those who refused to forgive. Peter had his answer: Forgive every time! If we do not, we will pay dearly according to God's will. Perhaps, Peter understood it to mean that if we hold out, waiting to be paid back for the wrongs done to us, we will be the ones who ultimately pay.

If, on the other hand, we cancel the debts owed to us, we will be set free. It is like drinking poison and expecting it to kill someone else, I'm sure we know better. Any negative reaction to this parable reveals that we are naive. Rightly so, from our perspective, we have every right to hold out and hold on, until we are paid back, but, from God's perspective, it is possibly the most self-destructive thing we can do. There may not be a literal prison for those who harbor resentment in their hearts, but we certainly put ourselves in a prison of sorts when we cling to the debts owed to us by others.

Perhaps that is what Jesus had in mind when he gave such a stern warning; if we demand payment, we will pay. Jesus' warning is severe because the consequences of ignoring it are severe. Unresolved anger has multigenerational implications.

Jesus exemplified forgiveness and his warning is not an exaggeration! That is what we should expect from a Savior who came to earth to rescue us from sin, its penalty, and its power and who will ultimately save us from the PRESENCE of sin! Glory Hallelujah! Beloved, our pains are not trophies to show off. It is not a story to tell but a potential poison to our souls if not appropriately channeled. To refuse to forgive is to choose to self-destruct! May that not be our portion in Jesus Christ's name! Amen.

The Full Circle of Forgiveness

Until we see forgiveness as a circle, we will miss the deeper meaning of the parable of the ungrateful servant. I believe Peter possibly did not grab the full meaning until months later when he found himself staring at Jesus hanging from a Roman cross. If this was the price of his forgiveness then who was he to withhold forgiveness from others?

God's decision to forgive Peter required the death of His son; Peter's decision to forgive those who had offended him would cost him little more than his pride. This is the same with us all, in the shadow of our hurt, forgiveness feels like a decision to reward the offender. But, in the shadow of the *Cross*, forgiveness is merely a gift from one undeserving soul to another. Forgiveness is the gift that ensures my freedom from the prison of bitterness and resentment.

When we accept forgiveness from God, we are set free from the penalty of our sin. When we extend forgiveness to our adversaries, there is a sense in which we are set free from their sins as well. This I also believe is the force behind the last phrase in Paul's exhortation:

> "Be kind and compassionate to one another, forgiving each other, just as in Christ God forgave you" (Ephesian 4:32).

The kind of forgiveness Paul was talking about does not make any sense unless you are a forgiven person. He was confident and felt free to command the believers in Ephesus to forgive unconditionally because he was writing to Christians; men and women who themselves had experienced the forgiveness of God through Christ.

Most people who are hesitant to forgive others are invariably evaluating their decision based on what was done "to" them, rather than what was done "for" them; there is a big difference. Perspective is everything! As a believer, I am called and liberated to view forgiveness through the lens of the cross. Like the servant in Jesus' parable, he was forgiven for a debt he could never repay, the least he could have done was to cancel the debt owed him by his fellow servant, that is what it means to forgive" just as" God forgave us all.

Christ-followers are not expected to treat others the way they have been treated; they are called to treat people the way they have been treated by our father in heaven. I do not forgive because others deserve it, I forgive because I have been forgiven fully, finally, freely.

Forgive and Keep on Forgiving

The Apostle used a present continuous tense here. It was not a one-time action. His use of the term "forgive" indicates a mindset, attitude, habit, way of life, or what we call second nature. For us believers, it should be a way of life if we are to commit to keeping our hearts free of anger and bitterness. It is the first line of defense in the face of hurt, disappointment, betrayal, and rejection.

In Paul's days, there were two different words in the Greek language used to express the concept of forgiveness. The word Apostle Paul chose for this admonition conveys the idea of forgiveness as a "gift" We must give it out constantly, in season or out of season. Specifically, we are called to cancel debts as fast as they are incurred.

Forgiveness runs so contrary to our sense of justice and fairness so it is highly unlikely that we would ever "feel" like forgiving. But in the Bible, forgiveness is never presented as a feeling; it is always described as a decision. Forgiveness is a gift we decide to give despite how we feel!

Four phases MUST take place to complete the circle of overcoming anger in our lives:

- Identify who we are angry with
- Determine what they owe us
- Cancel the debt
- Dismiss the case.

It is good to forgive. Forgiving is not evidence of weakness; on the contrary, it is a sign of physical and emotional maturity.

Un-forgiveness ties us to the past, debases the present, and hinders the future. **"Un-forgiveness is a prison that cages destiny and puts its victims in the depression box. Un-forgiveness damages our joy and bitterness sets in. It is a pit and the only way out is to use the ladder of forgiveness to climb out. It takes humility and maturity to forgive. Forgiveness is a spiritual medicine that heals the soul and gives us sound minds".**

Identify who we are Angry with- The Offender

Habit #2- Confronting Anger

Forgiveness is more than just a decision to move on with our lives and forget the past. Trying to "forget" debt is not the same as canceling it. Make a list of those who have mistreated or taken advantage of us, going back as far as you can recall. Believe that the Holy Spirit will bring them to your remembrance because God is interested in setting us free for His glory since we are made in His image. One mistake we make is assuming we have forgiven someone just because we "put it behind us", so to speak.

- Who do you wish to never see again?
- Who do you see yourself having an imaginary conversation with?
- Who would you like to pay back if you thought you could get away with it?
- Who do you secretly desire to see fail?

Here is a list to help us get started: Family, Friends, ex-boyfriend or girlfriend, ex-husband or wife, deceased parents, work associates, coaches, and bosses. Even people we may not know their names hurt us in unforgettable ways. I know it is not easy but it's very vital for our freedom. This is an opportunity to purge our hearts of the junk that has been hindering the relationships we value most; it's worth the effort. Yes, it is indeed.

Identify what they owe you–Be Specific

These sayings are true "you cannot confront what you cannot identify" and "you cannot conquer what you cannot confront". Most of us would rather skip this phase. As a result, we forgive "generally" but not specifically.

This is where the parable of the ungrateful servant is so helpful. Just as the king forgave the "specific" amount owed him by the servant, so we must determine exactly what is owed to us by those who have hurt us. You know what the person who hurt you "did" but what exactly did they "take"? Until we know the answer to this important question, we will not be ready to forgive. We may go through the motions of forgiveness but experience no freedom. We have heard these comments several times, "But I have already forgiven him/her". Usually, this is spoken with such intensity that it is obvious forgiveness has not taken place. Generic forgiveness does not heal specific hurts.

We must pinpoint what was taken from us. What do the people on our list owe us? What did they take from us? What would they need to return to put things back the way they were? Is it an apology, money, time, marriage, family, job, reputation repair, an opportunity, a promotion, or a chapter of your life? To be specific, we cannot cancel a debt we have not identified.

Cancel the Debt!

This phase is non-negotiable! After we have identified exactly what was taken, we 'must' cancel the debt. That means deciding that the offending party does not owe us anything anymore! Glory Alleluia! Just as Christ canceled our sinful debt at Calvary, so we must cancel the debt that others have incurred against us. This may be a simple decision you make quietly in your heart or something you may want to mark with a tangible item.

I read in Dr. Charles Stanley's Book, 'The Gift of Forgiveness' how he marked the day he forgave his stepfather. He sat across from an empty chair and spoke as if his stepfather were present. He recounted all offenses he held against his stepfather through the years and then declared him forgiven. When he finished the 'conversation', he stood up, walked away, and was able to leave his anger and resentments behind. Whenever "Satan" began to stir up those feelings, he would remind Satan that his stepfather no longer owed him, and the debt was canceled.

I have also heard how others dealt with this by listing 'what was owed'. They put the list in an envelope and burned it, and thus declared those debts canceled. Others buried their list or nailed their list to a cross as a reminder that Christ had suffered for those sins as well. I believe there are benefits or advantages of physicalizing your decision to forgive. This can be especially helpful not only for those whose hurt has happened in the past, but for those daily offenses we incur, a quick, simple, but specific declaration is all it takes.

Here is an example:

'Dear Heavenly, Gracious and Merciful Father, _____ has taken _____ from me and I have held on to this debt long enough. I choose to cancel this debt. _____ does not owe me anymore. Just as you forgave me, I forgive _____ in Jesus' name. Amen.

It is not necessary to tell the person that you have forgiven them, because in many cases the offending parties may not feel as if they have done anything wrong, to begin with. Sharing our decision to forgive could be taken as an accusation.

But when the offending party asks for forgiveness or returns to apologize for an incident from the past, it is always appropriate to tell them our decision to cancel the debt. Otherwise, the decision is between us and God.

Dismiss the Case

Here the narrative or story of Joseph in the Bible helps us to understand this final phase in the process of forgiveness! The process centers on a daily decision not to 'reopen' the case. What makes this phase so difficult is that our 'feelings' do not automatically follow our decision to forgive. Besides, forgiving someone does not erase our 'memories'. I wish it did; that would mean to forgive and

Habit #2- Confronting Anger

forget would be much easier. But in most cases, no sooner have we forgiven than something happens to remind us of the offense all over again and again. Once our memories are triggered, the old feelings come flooding back.

There are two options here when this happens:

- We take hold of the offense all over again, crack up the imaginary conversation and reopen our case.
- We try not to think about it and turn our thoughts elsewhere.

Neither response is appropriate or helpful at all.

Thank God there is a third option that works; when those memories of the past hurt flood our minds, we must go ahead and face them. Allow yourself to remember the incident, it is ok to feel the emotions those memories elicit. But instead of reopening the case against our offender, we take that opportunity to restate and affirm our decision; "He or she doesn't owe me anymore, I have canceled the debt!" We then proceed to thank our heavenly father for giving us the grace and strength to forgive.

Please do not accept the lies that you have not forgiven the offender. Just like in the case of Joseph, the offending parties may be the ones trying to reopen or restate the offense. But we must be intentional by simply focusing on the truth that the debt has been canceled. Period! And how do we know? We know because we decided, as an act of our will to cancel it. Feelings come and feelings go, but the decision remains, "He or she does not owe me anymore".

There are no problems with our memories, our memories are not our enemies. Memories are simply memories, a natural tendency to recollect the past, but what we do with them determines their impact, positively or negatively.

We must note that "truly forgiving" does not always equate to "truly forgetting". It is tempting to judge whether we have forgiven the offender by how we feel toward the offender. But our 'feelings' towards someone are not as accurate a gauge as we need them to be. Our feelings are generally the last things to come to terms with. In time, if we cling to the fact that this offender does not owe us anymore, our 'feelings' will change. The day will come when we will be able to respond to the offender, considering where he or she stands with Christ, rather than considering how the offender treated us.

Impossibilities of Payback

One may ask if it is wrong to want to be paid back for what was taken. I believe the answer is No. There is nothing wrong with wanting to be repaid. The problem is that in most cases, it is practically impossible to be reimbursed for what was taken. But let's not confuse payback with restitution. Payback is wanting something in return for what you have lost; restitution is the offender owning up to what he did to you and being willing to make amends.

Jesus made it clear in His parable: The King who forgave the servant's debt was going to lose a lot of money regardless of how he handled the situation. The servant owed the King far more than he would be able to repay in his lifetime. Restitution was completely out of the question. Selling the servant's wife, children and possessions would not still have been enough. So, it is with us, when asked what it will take to make things right, it suddenly dawns on us that the debt owed cannot be paid!

How can a man who abandoned his children ever really replace what he has taken from them? How can a child who made their parent's life painful or hellish for years give back what they have taken? How can a spouse who cheated on his or her partner ever restore all that was taken? Sincerely, how do you restore time and affection? How does a mother pay back her grown-up child for not being there for him or her?

We cannot pay back a missing relationship; we cannot replace a damaged reputation, and there is no way to make up for years of criticism and neglect. How does someone pay back or give back innocence and purity? Once violated, these and so many debts cannot be repaid. The only logical thing to do is simply cancel it. The truth remains, that nothing can make up for the past.

There is an emotional element involved in the hurt that cannot be compensated with apologies, promises, or even financial restitution. Just like the case of insurance payments due to death, an apology or a check does not erase the experience.

To some degree, there will always be an outstanding debt. To pursue or wait for 'payback' is just futile because it can't and most likely won't happen. To insist on it is to set ourselves up for unnecessary predictable heartbreaks. To cling to hurt while waiting to be repaid is to allow the seed of bitterness to take root and grow. When that happens, we end up allowing the offender to hurt us repeatedly.

In my healthcare background, even more, as a critical/emergency room nurse, when the doctor tells someone that they have a bad heart or that they have heart disease, the individual's overriding concerns are about how it can be fixed. How it happened or whose is at fault are secondary concerns at that point.

We should be driven by a similar concern when it comes to the anger and bitterness that pollutes our hearts. Blaming will not make our hearts better and holding out for an apology will not suffice. The cure is forgiveness. You may need to spend some time dealing with unfinished business from the past; hopefully, the four-process path outlined earlier will help facilitate that.

But in a world where neglect, insensitivity, and injustice are the norm rather than the exception, forgiveness must become a habit worth cultivating. Of all the monstrous forces, I believe unresolved anger from intentional and unintentional hurt is the most devastating, and yet it is the most ignored even though the easiest to overcome.

So the solution is that we simply make up our minds to cancel the debt. We decide to declare that the offender does not owe us anymore.

Let us recap!!

> "Then Peter came to Jesus and asked, "Lord, how many times shall I forgive my brother when he sins against me, up to seven times?" Jesus answered, "I tell you, not seven times, but seventy times seven" (Matthew 18:21-22).

Now to say that we will forgive but not forget means that we invariably nurse old wounds and allow ourselves to be poisoned by bitterness and hatred. Although forgiving and forgetting are two different processes, we must aim to have the entire spectrum completed. To forget is not to cease to remember what was done at all, it is to cease to hold the offender accountable. Sadly, we do not realize the damage we are doing to ourselves when we foster disputes that should have been buried decades ago. Simmering hatred and growing bitterness have disastrous effects on the one who harbors them.

Our spirits become small, we grieve and quench the Holy Spirit, and eventually, our thoughts become twisted.

Nothing is seen in its true perspective anymore and our attitudes become petty and warped.

No one can afford to accommodate an unforgiving spirit. Its companion is hatred and together they cause unhappiness and internal defeat. Christ's teachings were not unrealistic or removed from the hard facts of daily life, especially regarding forgiveness.

If we agree with what Christ taught in principle but still 'feel' that it is beyond our ability to forgive; just remember that Jesus not only calls us to live right but He enables us to do what we can't do with our strength. The Holy Spirit equips us to do just that.

May I also add, that it has been proven in medicine that some physical sicknesses are triggered off by anger and bitterness? There is the story of a man who had a stroke and when he did a retrospective evaluation, he was able to find out that he suffered the stroke after he became very angry with someone.

Chapter Thirteen

Habit #3–Confronting Greed!

Greed says, 'I owe me'. The person whose heart is coated with greed believes he or she earned the good things that have come their way. Therefore, they are so determined to control their possessions and wealth. Greedy people have a supersized sense of ownership. But unbeknownst to most greedy people, greed is fueled by fear.

Once we peel back all the excuses and the endless 'but what if?' scenarios, we will discover a heart so full of FEAR- (False Evidence Appearing Real). Specifically, this individual has a fear that God either cannot or will not take care of them. So greedy individuals set out to acquire and maintain everything they need to provide the sense of security they desire.

But like all human appetites, the appetite for financial security can never be fully satisfied. There is never enough money. So, the acquisition, hoarding, and self-indulgence continue. Well, is there anything wrong with saving for the eventuality of life? No, there is nothing particularly wrong with acquiring things, and therein lies the challenge of identifying greed.

Greedy people do not want their children to feel the financial burden of caring for them when they are older, and there is certainly nothing wrong with that. Maybe greed is good, you be the judge of that.

In Luke 12:15, Jesus began His discourse on greed with a warning. He knew back then what we are just beginning to discover. Greed can take residence in our hearts and live there undetected for very long. The unguarded heart is highly susceptible to this debilitating 'disease'. It is exceedingly difficult to diagnose or self-diagnose, extremely hard indeed.

Jesus goes on to uncover the lie that fuels all greed saying, "Life doesn't consist in the abundance of possession". Some individuals believe that their lives can be judged by what they own; their life is pretty much the total of their possessions and many of us today are prone to this belief.

Jesus continues with the parable of a wealthy landowner whose property yielded a much larger crop than he had expected or needed. What was supposed to be a good fortune left him with a dilemma: he had no place to store his bountiful harvest. Then he thought to himself, 'What do I do?' I have no place to store my crops.' In other words, 'What am I to do with all the stuff that I have because of all my hard work?' The landowner had no place to 'store' his crops; that is the farmer's talk for 'saving'. What he needed was a place to 'hoard' his reserves.

In an agricultural society, it would be immediately obvious that the abundance of this man's harvest had little to do with his hard work. Farmers are always at the mercy of factors that they have no control over. But the greedy man or woman does not see the world that way. To them, whatever comes their way do so because they have earned it.

And since the landowner believed he earned this abundance, he never considers the notion that God might have had anything to do with it. Even if he had credited this bounty as God's blessing, it never crossed his mind that the extra he has been blessed with wasn't intended just for his consumption alone.

God had provided this farmer with 'extra.' The Question the farmer should have asked was, 'Lord, what do you want me to do with this extra supply?' This is a true question that we all should ask God from time to time. We, to some extent, are all guilty of this farmer's mistake. We say to ourselves, "Wow, lucky me!" Then we hoard our returns; after all, we earned every penny. This was exactly what this farmer or landowner decided to do: He said,

> "This is what I will do, I will tear down my barns and build bigger ones, and there I will store my surplus grain, and I will say

to myself, you have plenty of grain laid up
for many years, take life easy; eat, drink
and be merry" (Luke 12:18-19).

Bigger barns? Yes sir, what a brilliant idea! That will certainly solve everything; he will be set for life. So, he thought. This type of thinking is common among those whose hearts are damaged by greed. We do not need to look far to see that this is a common malady. Think about all the mini-warehouses/storage units all around us that are used by people who have stuff that cannot fit into their homes. Those things are just piles of junk. Junk that could have been liquidated when it was worth something and turned into cash to put to good use on behalf of those who do not have enough. But no, we decide to rent a 'bigger barn'. Guess why? Because someday, maybe we might need that stuff. So, just because of that 'someday' that we might need it, we decided to store or hoard it!

After declaring his intention to build bigger barns, the landlord explains why he has chosen to pursue this course of action. Keep in mind; that greed is always looking for something 'good' to hide behind. For instance, this man has decided to build bigger barns to secure his future so he can have all he needs to be met for many years to come. Nothing wrong with that. We can call that disciplined planning and opportunistic saving. We could even say he was being proactive!

Well, Jesus did not see it that way.

Thank God that Jesus can see our motives and true intentions because left to our mindsets, we would consider this landowner a great role model! Yes, the landowner planned but he did not plan 'far' enough ahead. Yes, he truly needed to consider his future but not in the way he thought. He was projecting for years he did not have. Just as he overlooked the God factor when evaluating his good agricultural fortune, the landowner also overlooked the God factor when counting how many years he had left. He equated his abundance of stuff to an assurance of an abundance of time, but the two do not have anything to do with each other. The very day the landowner decided to keep everything he had earned, he lost it, or maybe it would be more accurate to say, 'it lost him'.

Just after this man's thought process was completed, he got the shocking news: he was going to die sometime that night. He was about to learn the hard way that his life was not equivalent to the number of his possessions; He would eventually run out of time before he ran out of stuff.

We can see that the landowner was more dependent on God than he realized. He was entirely reliant on God for his allotment of time, too bad he did not see that he was equally dependent on God for his allotment of stuff.

Sadly, with the bad news for the landowner came a question that is loaded with implications for each of us today. God said to him,

> "You fool! This night your life will be demanded from you, then who will get what you have prepared for yourself?" (Luke 12:20).

The obvious answer is 'someone else'. Someone else will end up with everything the landowner had 'earned', 'deserved', and consequently stored up. Someone else will end up with the very stuff the landowner had hoarded for himself when he should have depended on God's provision. In the end, all his possessions will be distributed to others, not because he was generous, but because he died; such an irony.

This parable of the rich foolish landowner directs our attention to an obvious but often overlooked reality. Eventually, everything we claim to own will be owned by someone else, and in the end, it will all be given away. So, to assume that everything that comes our way is for our consumption is shortsighted and 'foolish'. It is not a matter of 'if' somebody else will get it; it is just a matter of 'when' and 'how'. Either we give it away while we still have time, or it is taken away when our time runs out.

And Jesus our savior closes His parable with a stern warning:

> "This is how it will be with whoever stores up things for themselves, but is not rich towards God" (Luke 12:21).

So here we see the Biblical definition of a greedy person: A person who stores up things for himself or herself but is not rich towards God. Being rich toward God is being generous to those in need. A greedy person is a man or woman who saves carefully but gives sparingly.

What is the warning this parable is conveying to us? What exactly will happen to us if we are generous savers but not generous givers? Death? Not really. The real moral of the story is that those whose eagerness to store up material goods outpaces their willingness to give will suffer a complete and total loss when their time runs out.

The landowner suffered a complete and total reversal of fortune at the point of death. He lost everything in this life and had nothing to show for it in the next. He did not only lose his life but he also lost everything he considered 'life'. He was rich in this world but poor toward God because everything that came his way was used for his private consumption. That's why Jesus called him a fool. The sad truth was that he failed to acknowledge God in his life while he had time until his time ran out. We are not told how many opportunities came his way to put God where He deserves to be in his life but one can safely assume that he had several opportunities in the past but squandered them all until this final moment.

Sadly, we would have envied him, a fool that believed that an abundance of stuff meant an abundance of time. He was a fool to assume that his good fortune was the direct result of his hard work. He was a fool not to give to the less fortunate from his abundance, knowing that the day would come when everything would be taken from him, including any further opportunity to be generous.

In some parts of the world where kidnapping for ransom is rampant, the kidnappers would call the victim's family members saying "Your money or his life". We all know what to do when cases like that make a demand on us, but not when God does.

This parable of the rich foolish landowner does two important things for us all. First, it defines greed from God's perspective. Second, it offers a simple remedy. The problem with God's definition from a humanity standpoint is that it is a bit broader than most of us are comfortable with. God's solution is practical; anyone can practice it. Simply put, 'Habit is the solution'. A habit that has the power to free our greed-ridden hearts.

Generosity

In consumer-driven culture or society, we must learn to separate potential possessions and income from our actual possessions and income. This begs the question, why do we have so much?

We live in a culture that keeps us laser-focused on what we do not have and focusing on what we do not have leaves our hearts vulnerable to greed. If we are on a quest for more, then when more does come along, we assume it is for us alone. If we are living for the next purchase or the next upgrade, we are consuming mentally what we hope to soon consume physically. We are anticipating our future consumption.

That kind of attitude leaves us with little margin to be generous. And before we know it, we start building bigger barns or bigger garages or renting bigger storage spaces. Recall in the parable that the wealthy landowner believed he deserved it and he did not recognize the divine providence behind his bountiful harvest.

Assuming we are as shortsighted as the rich landowner, I believe we must always stop to ask, why God has provided us with more than we need. This is worth giving some consideration. Take me as an example. In the past, when I did not have enough, was I hesitant to question God about my lack? No, I sure was not. I was quick to let God know immediately that I have a need, with great expectation that God will provide, and I thanked God when He provided and shared testimonies about the goodness of God. So now that I have more than enough, I believe it is exactly right to also question God about the use of the surplus. As humans, when we do not have enough, we wonder why; then why not wonder when we have more than enough?

Surplus: Blessing or Curse

Looking at some countries in Africa which I will leave un-named, an assessment of the natural resources they have should make them the richest nations in the world. But alas, they are among the poorest nations despite their abundant natural resources. One begins to wonder whether there is a curse that follows blessings. In my native country, before the discovery of oil in 1957, we were self-sufficient as producers of cash crops and other agricultural products. Our economy was strong and buoyant and our currency was at par with the pound. But as soon as oil was discovered what ought to be a blessing became the bane of our country. Today oil has become a curse rather than a blessing!

In analyzing the issue of Surplus (supply with a plus), the parable of the rich fool makes it all too clear why we have more than we need. Before we head down the path of predictability, here is a thought we should consider: What might be the reason why God is providing us with more than our daily bread? Perhaps it's to ensure our children have everything they need, or maybe not.

History has proven that leaving our children with a lot of money generally does not set them up to be successful in life.

At the same time, I do not think God gave us resources to ruin our children's lives. We have also seen cases where abundance or accumulated assets create more family wars and no peace. The more people have the more they worry about their wealth and feel the need to do whatever it takes to guard what they have.

What about God providing us with extra to elevate our standard of living? After all, that is the American dream! At this point, I say a big thank you to the credit card industry which has made many of us live lifestyles that obviously outpace our income and we are continually urged not to lag too far behind the "Jones". Buy now, pay later has become the norm rather than the exception to the norm and there is a booming industry behind it all.

The result today is artificially induced financial pressure. One might argue that their financial concerns do not feel artificial, since the costs associated with maintaining the lifestyle are very real; such as cable TV, phone bill, the credit card bill. Always remember, those bills exist because 'WE' have chosen to lead a lifestyle that keeps pace with (or outpaces) our income.

We have convinced ourselves that those Luxuries are necessities.

Well, I beg to differ, after having to live without all that for almost 10 years as a migrant from a developing country, I know firsthand that it is possible to survive within your means. We have inflated our sense of what is essential and have created huge financial pressure. It is an artificial pressure, which can easily be alleviated by rearrangement of our lifestyle. Just throttle back, scale back and the pressure will subside.

Where our spending habits do not give us any margin financially, there is no way to avoid avarice. When the pressure is on, we have little choice but to think of ourselves first and that is the essence of greed. You do not need to have 'extra' to be greedy. If we plan to spend whatever comes our way on ourselves, then this is a recipe for greed. Once we allow our lifestyles to keep in lockstep with or surpass our incomes, we will find it near impossible to keep greed from taking root in our hearts.

Early Retirement: Blessing or Curse

In Western Culture, it is common to retire early but in developing countries retirement whether early or not means something completely different. It means going back to one's roots, serving, and adding value to one's communities with their time, talent, and treasure. It involves sharing a wealth of wisdom with the upcoming generation and expending remains days of their life with tangible footprints in the society.

In the parable of the rich landowner, the early retirement was not his idea, it just happened to him. Perhaps, God provided him with extra so he can retire early but just as it never crossed his mind to be generous with his harvest, it didn't occur to him to be generous with his time.

Time can only be expended in three ways: Spend it, waste it, or invest it. Each option has its consequential outcome that is beyond our control. We chose our actions but not the consequences. Luke 12:19 says,

> "And I will say to myself, you have plenty of grain laid up for many years take life easy, eat, drink and be merry".

There is nothing wrong with cashing out of a company due to a combination of hard work and good fortune. The problem comes when God is completely out of the equation. In the verse above, see how many times the rich landowner referred to 'himself'. He simply failed to recognize that God had not just freed up his time only to eat, drink, and be merry. He did not understand that his 'free' time was a resource to be invested responsibly with great dividends in the kingdom of God for humanity.

We certainly have a lot of great men and women in our society that have been using their 'free' time and resources to fund strategic ministries all over the world. This is simply because they asked the fundamental question; why did God provide me with more than I need? And then got the right answer or at least it became clear with time. So, if God is filling up our barns faster than we anticipated, it may be so God is leading us out of the marketplace or job earlier than we planned, into our 'work' where we cannot retire, or lay off till Jesus' returns.

One thing I learned from the Late Rev Dave Pawson, British Theologian, and Bible Teacher, is that there ought not to be a distinction between the secular and the spiritual. Every work we find ourselves doing whether in the house of God or our secular environment is spiritual because it should be unto the Lord.

We must ask God why? Why do I have more 'time' and 'resources' than I need? Pray for the grace to wait and with time it will become clear. When our time eventually runs out, we will have something to show for it in eternity. We will be rich towards God. Amen.

Overcoming Greed!

For those of us who grew up with siblings, I'm sure we all can recall that famous word 'share' used so often by our parents. We in turn teach our children to 'share' because watching someone eat two cookies in the presence of someone who has none does not seem right, does it? No, it does not, and we feel compelled to say or do something. Perhaps that is why Jesus said,

> "Give to the one who asks you and does not turn away from the one who wants to borrow from you" (Matthew 5:42).

Imagine if we all could see from the lens of this verse. Those who have 'two cookies' would give to those who have none. Embracing this simple truth is the key to ridding our hearts of greed.

Remember:

- Guilt is conquered with a confession
- Anger is conquered with forgiveness
- Greed is conquered with generosity.

I dare you to try giving. Generosity will break the grip of greed on our lives. So, whether we think we have extra or not, let us begin to give and give generously, to the point that it forces us to adjust our lifestyle. That means, if we are not giving, according to Jesus, to the point that it changes our lifestyles, we are 'greedy'. Also, if we consume to the point of having little or nothing left to give, we are 'greedy'. If we consume and save to the point that there is little or nothing to give, we are 'greedy'.

Some of us may not fit into the examples above. Maybe we feel compassion every time we see someone in need, and in our hearts, we do want to help, we genuinely want to give, but we cannot. So, is it fair to say in this case that 'greed' is the culprit? Yes. Because greed is not a feeling, it's a refusal to act. We can feel compassion toward people in need and be as stingy as Scrooge. Greed is shown not by how we feel but by what we do with our feelings. Generous feelings and good intentions without action do not compensate for a greedy heart. Good intentions and greed can cohabit in our hearts for an exceptionally long time; sometimes indefinitely.

This is what makes this covert enemy such a threat to our hearts. We may never 'feel' it the way we do anger, guilt, or even jealousy but it is there anyway, it is dangerous, and it can lead to a total loss.

Keep First thing first!

Just as we cannot wait until we are in shape to start exercising, we must not wait until our 'fear' of giving is gone, to start giving. Do not wait until God changes your heart to give. Giving is the way God chooses to change our hearts, and as our hearts change, our attitudes, and feelings will follow.

God loves a cheerful giver, but He will put our money, time, and resources to godly use whether we are cheerful or not. So let us give until we get cheerful.

Again, our giving must impact our lifestyle if it is going to break the power of greed. The best way to do that is to become a percentage giver; this is a simple place to start. Percentage giving involves giving away a percentage of everything we receive, right off the top, as soon as we get them. Specifically, the first check we would write after depositing our paycheck can be a check to an organization that supports the work of the kingdom; this is how we can become rich towards God.

In the bible times, there was no such organization; believers simply gave to their place of worship and the poor. Praise God that we now have multiple options.

Simply choose one or two to start and start now! Writing this check or sending this contribution 'first' ensures that God's kingdom is funded ahead of ours. It is in keeping with Matthew 6:33,

> "But seek first the kingdom of God and his righteousness, and all these things shall be added to you."

It means we must live on the 'leftovers' for a change. I believe we can start with as low as 2%, and then believe God as we bump it up time after time (with 10 or 12 % as a goal to reach or exceed). Certainly, giving at this level is evidence of a lifestyle adjustment, but percentage giving is just a great place to start- just the beginning.

We must pray to be spontaneous givers as well. When we see someone in need, we give. Isn't that what we expect God to do for us when we are in need? Let us make the first move. If we have extra and somebody is in need, share, that's what our extra is there for. These two habits: percentage giving and spontaneous giving will protect us from Greed.

The day will come when we receive an unexpected windfall and our first thought will be 'who can we help' or what kingdom endeavor can I be part of? At that very moment, we will know that through the habit of generous giving, we have broken the power of greed in our lives. Amen. It is a habit that changes everything.

We Choose Our Action Not the Consequence

Yes! It has been said, "The love of money is the 'root' of all evil". Also, money 'answers' all things. There is no ministerial gifting that would not require money because it is the only real currency of exchange we have under the sun. We do not need money in heaven, just like it was never needed in the Garden of Eden but we sure do need it now. So, having money is not necessarily a bad thing, it is not knowing the 'why' behind the money that is the cause of all the problems we have with money. Whether we are beneficiaries of hard work, good business sense, savvy investment, a family inheritance, or just plain blessings, there is no reason to feel bad about having a lot of money. Besides, it is not really 'our' money anyways:

> "And you shall remember the Lord your God, for it is He who gives you the power to get wealth, that..." Deuteronomy 8:18).

One thing is abundantly clear; we are not owners but managers. And yes, some people get to manage more than others. Some of us are better stewards or managers than others. We can only name three ways to expend money: Waste, spend or invest. Remember also the parable of the talents, so we should never feel guilty for what we have received, but we should have a deep sense of responsibility.

Be responsible! God owns everything,

> "Yours Lord, is the greatness and the power and the glory and the majesty and the splendor for everything in heaven and earth is Yours. Yours lord, is the Kingdom; You are exalted as head over all". (1 Chronicle 29:11).

Guilt will only be a factor if we have not come to grasp the concept of ownership versus management. Examine the financial manager or money manager, when you sit with them the very first question they ask is: what are your goals? Because they are handling and managing your money, their personal goals are irrelevant. All good financial or money managers will handle your money with your goals in mind and be responsible for it without feeling guilty.

In conclusion, we must come to terms now with the idea that we are just managers of someone else's (God's) assets. With this recognition comes a freedom that 'owners' never experience. We will be ultimately free from fear of loss in this life and more concerned with avoiding total loss in the life to come.

Chapter Fourteen

Habit #4- Confronting Jealousy

*E*very one of the four invaders of the heart is fueled by the notion that someone owes somebody something, and it is this debt dynamic that gives each of these monsters their power. Regardless of who owes what to whom, if someone's holding on to debt, there will be tension in such a relationship.

Guilt says "I owe you", so the solution is confession. Anger is fueled by the notion, "you owe me", so that debt is remedied with forgiveness. Greed is kept alive by the assumption that I owe myself, a twisted way of thinking that is remedied through generous giving. Then Jealousy says God owes me!

From the beginning of time, jealousy has played a feature role in the story of human relationships. Cain was jealous of Abel, Esau was jealous of Jacob, and Joseph's brothers were jealous of their younger brother's relationship with their father. We all have our experiences. When we think of jealousy; we think of the things other people have that we lack; looks, talent, health, height, money, connections, and so on. And so, we think we have a problem with the person who possesses what we lack. But as we said earlier, we believe God should have fixed all of that.

Whatever God has given to my neighbor, He could have chosen to give me as well, right? Bottom line; if only God had taken care of us the way God took care of our neighbors (the people we know), we would be in much better shape relationally, professionally, and financially.

We would say our real problem is not with the people whose stuff we envy; it is with the creator – God who owes me! So, I am holding a grudge against God. Until we face this simple truth, jealousy will continue to terrorize our lives and wreak havoc in our relationships. The good news is, this behemoth, like the other three (heart issues) has a vulnerability and it is something we might never expect.

Truth be told, the driving force behind jealousy is the driving force behind every single struggle we will encounter on this side of heaven. From marriage problems to personnel problems in our workplace, all of them can be traced or reduced to one common issue. This issue encompasses and explains the rifts caused by guilt, anger, and greed too. Understanding this one dynamic will free us and help us quit blaming everything and everybody for our less than attractive behavior.

The Root Cause of Jealousy

In the book of James, the half-brother of our Lord and Savior Jesus Christ, writing in Chapter 4, James asked the question: What causes fights and quarrels among us? We can all look around, in our churches, places of employment, family, and homes. The answer to this question would seem to be as varied as the fight and quarrels themselves.

Disagreements and arguments are caused by any number of circumstances, right? Well, the Apostle James differs here. He peels back the circumstantial excuses and goes right to the heart of the matter–the common denominator for every struggle we had or will ever have: "What causes fights and quarrels among us? Don't they come from our desires that battle within us?" James believes that our external conflicts are the direct result of an internal conflict that has worked its way to the surface.

The word 'desires' here means pleasures. This same Greek word is translated as 'pleasure' later in this chapter. James believes also that if we find ourselves in an argument, it will be because a battle within us has spilled out onto the surface.

According to James, conflicting desires are churning around inside one of us, and if we bump each other too hard, what's on the inside is going to spill out. The saying is true; the people we hurt the most are those we claim to love the most. These are the people who birthed us, raised us, and exchanged vows with us. So, why them of all people?

The answer is that they are close to us. When we can no longer contain the conflict raging within us, it spills out on those closest to us, even if they are innocent bystanders. The common denominator in all our relational conflicts is us.

Can we always get what we want?

What is the thing that causes this internal struggle, threatening the peace of every family, and place of employment, tormenting our relationships? James said: "you want something but don't get it". Simply put, we cannot get what we want, we cannot have our way.

The term 'want' as used here carries the force of 'yearn for', 'lust for', or 'strongly desire.' We see this type of argument between women all the time. James says the same is true of every adult conflict. In the face of these conflicts, what do we do? We do whatever we have to do to get what we want (You desire but do not have, so you kill, you covet but you cannot get what you want, so you quarrel and fight. James 4:2). 'Kill' in this verse may be a hyperbole, but let us face it; most murders we read or know about were perpetrated by somebody who wanted something.

Even more to the point, most murderers had personal relationships with their victims. Investigators always begin their investigation with family and so-called friends.

Habit #4- Confronting Jealousy

Now! If we have been mad enough to hurt someone, it was because that person did not give us our due, and we did not get what we wanted. 'Covert' means to hotly pursue or to strive after.

The picture painted is of someone who's constantly trying to meet a need that cannot be met because in the end, 'we cannot always get what we want. Yes, there are times we get what we want but looking beneath the surface there are desires that are constantly swirling around our hearts, the hunger that is never fully and finally satisfied. Just like with food, we may feel full after a meal but three hours later we headed back to the kitchen for more, because we have an appetite by nature that is never fully and finally satisfied. It is only temporarily quelled, so no matter how full we feel after a meal, we do not give up eating.

The desires described here by Apostle James represent unquenchable thirsts. Our thirst for stuff, money, recognition, success, progress, intimacy, sex, fun, relationship and partnership is insatiable. We never get enough of any of these things to satisfy our desires fully and finally. As C.S. Lewis points out in "Mere Christianity" the more you feed an appetite, the more it escalates in intensity. 'Appetites grow through indulgence, not neglect'. Gluttons think just as much about food as starving people. People with power want more power, wealthy people want more money. Men and women who bounce from one partner to the next are never fully satisfied with any of them. The point is, that our desires and pleasures are not best dealt with by continually trying to satisfy them.

The futility of the Blame Game

The endless, fruitless attempts to satisfy our desires are the things that fuel our conflicts. Is it not true that every relational struggle we have ever experienced can be reduced to the other person's trying to satisfy an internal desire in a manner that conflicts with the way we were planning to satisfy our own? And so, we quarrel and fight, and just like with children, the issue in every quarrel becomes each of us wanting to get our way.

Owning that makes a huge difference. When everybody involved owns it, the problems usually evaporate. Until we are ready to own our share of the problem, we will always tend to blame the other person, and blaming never resolved anything. Blaming just simply feeds the problem, but until we can stop and realize the fact that our real problem is that we are not getting what we 'want', we would have no recourse but to blame the other party.

This may sound extreme but the real meaning of blame is 'an admission that I cannot be happy without your cooperation. To blame is to acknowledge dependence: 'If you do not act a certain way, I cannot be satisfied or content.'

If we take this to its logical extreme, it means we can never be happy until we can control the actions and reactions of everybody we come into contact with, including everybody in our lane and both adjacent lanes on the freeway. If this is the case, it would seem that we have no hope. The good news is there is always hope. But until we are willing to fully embrace this divine truth that Apostle James clearly explained to us, it would seem that we have no choice but to try to squeeze our happiness and contentment out of people around us.

The problem is they are trying to squeeze theirs out of us as well, and eventually, everybody suffocates. We end up walking away convinced that the problem is somebody else. We search for someone else who can fill us up fully and, in the busyness, and earnestness of our search, we never stop long enough to figure out what it is that we want.

The Divine Solution

What do we do with desires and appetites that can never be fully satisfied? Apostle James says we take them to the one who 'created the appetite and desires' in the first place.

'You do not have it because you do not ask God. In other words, we do not get what we want because we are asking the wrong person. Instead of burdening the people we love with desires they were not designed to fulfill in the first place, Apostle James instructs us to bring them to our Heavenly Father. It is as if God is saying to us, 'By the way, this whole thing could have been avoided if you would come to Me first, instead of trying to squeeze whatever it is you think you need out of the people around you. God created this appetite in the first place not to be filled by nobody. Not our siblings, our spouse, our Boss, our neighbors, not even our parents would do because they are mere humans, incapable of satisfying those appetites.

James says "Take them to God Almighty!" Amen. Among Christians, we hear things like; "I already did", "I already prayed and prayed about it", and usually what they mean is 'I prayed that God would change the heart of so and so that he will give me what I deserve'. Brethren that is not what Apostle James is talking about! He is suggesting something more powerful than asking God to change someone else so that we can get our way. James is instructing us to bring our deepest desires and unmet needs to the father. He is permitting us to pour out our hearts in an unfiltered conversation with our creator.

Even Apostle Peter echoes the same advice,

> "Cast all your anxiety on Him because He cares for you" 1 Peter 5:7.

Beloved 'all' means 'all'. So, bring every frustration and fear to God. There is nothing too big or small. 'I know I should not feel this way but…' 'I know this is petty but…' We do not have to begin our prayers with any of these 'but' statements. None of that is necessary. And here is why? If it is important to you, it is important to God and because we are important to God, what affects us concerns Him.

Every concern of ours, whether great or small, matters to our Heavenly Father because we all matter to Him. Whether it pertains to our lives, our careers, our marriages, our parenting, our children young or old, our finances, education, or even our appearances; just bring it to God, and keep on bringing it all to God until you find the peace to get off your knees and face the day, confident in the knowledge that God cares for you.

Once we confess to God that our root problem is that we are not getting our way, and once we have thoroughly and completely dumped our desires and anxieties on God, we will find it much easier to deal with the people in our lives. Regardless of whether they ever give us recognition, love, or the credit we deserve, we will find peace because we are no longer looking to these people to meet a need that only God can meet.

The all Good and Perfect Gift

Now! James also said that the reason why when we ask and we do not receive is, 'when you ask, you do not receive, because you ask with wrong motives, that you may spend what you get on your pleasure' James 4:3. That certainly takes all the fun out of it.

After He instructs us to bring all our desires to God, he then tells us that God may say no. This sounds like a contradiction, right? Here I must say a big Hallelujah to our living, all-knowing God of all flesh. In hindsight, I thank God for the "NOs" to some of my prayers! I bet you all would agree with me because our desires would have ruined us. God loves us too much to give us everything we ask for. He loves those around us too much to give them everything they ask for. But guess what? God still wants us to ask. God still wants us to bring it all to Him because He wants us to know Him as the source of all 'good and perfect things' and when God says no, He wants us to trust Him.

Let me illustrate this a little more. Imagine your 5-year-old son coming to you a saying "Daddy, I know you love me so please give me the keys to your Mercedes Benz car so I can take a drive around the block." Your answer to your son will be a resounding no because you love him and have his best interest at heart. You know if you oblige him you will be exposing him to danger so you say no. Now you will not be upset with him because he asked for your keys after all he is your son, will you?

It would be easier if God would come out and just say No, instead, most times He is silent and things just do not change. The Porsche car never shows up in the driveway, nobody offers us a record deal, and the old back injury still gives us trouble.

God is not going to finance our self-destructive search for meaning outside His will, plan, and purpose for us. He is the source of 'all' good and perfect things, not 'all' things wished-for. Still, God wants us to ask, to learn to depend on and to cry out to him. God wants us to take and accept His 'No' as a definite answer instead of taking matters into our own hands. This is not always easy I must confess, but it is the best option.

James said in James chapter 1:7,

> "Every good and perfect gift is from above, coming down from the father of the heavenly lights, who does not change like shifting shadows".

Every good thing that comes our way comes from our Heavenly Father which is the very reason to take our unmet needs, our heartfelt desires, and even our embarrassing wants and wishes to God alone. At the end of the day, Mick Jagger was right; "You cannot always get what you want, nobody can, and it is not possible". Our appetite can never be fully satisfied.

The question is, are we going to continue anyway to try fulfilling our desire by wringing it out of the people around us or will we take it and leave it in the caring hands of our Father in Heaven? These are our only options. One leads to peace, the other to endless frustration.

Be on the look-out

It is easier for us to own up to anger than to own up to jealousy. Jealousy always seems and sounds petty, right? We can easily build up our case for our anger, but not jealousy, so we do not talk about it. But we sure 'feel' it.

Jealousy is dangerous. It is dangerous because it shapes our attitudes toward other people. It is hard to actively love someone we are jealous of. It is hard to serve (or submit to) someone who is a constant reminder of what we are not. Eventually, jealousy takes control of our attitudes towards people who have done nothing more than pull ahead of us in a race they are not even aware of. They have excelled in an area we have deemed important, and we hate them for it.

Another subtle phrase we use is 'I do not hate him or her, I just do not like or enjoy their company. So, without any real effort on our part, this jealousy becomes resentment. But resentment needs justification, so we go looking until we find it. I guarantee you that if you look hard enough you will find a reason.

There is a saying, "if you want to beat someone, you will always find a stick". Once we find a reason, we feel safe, there is no need to resolve our feelings because we know that they are perfectly justified in the human eyes. Sometimes we even rubber stamp our justification with the word of the scripture.

As sure as the sun rises, once our jealousy turns to resentment, it will know no bounds. It has the power to 'sour' our attitudes toward entire categories of individuals; rich people, supermodels, bodybuilders, mega-churches, pastors, stay-at-home moms, and career women, and it becomes easier to write off an entire swath of the human race.

Now, who are you jealous of or what category of people do you resent (within or outside our families)? Here are a few to get us started: professionals, performers, company executives, couples, singles, children, retirees, and so on. If we look, we will discover that our resentment, with all its shallow justifications, is just well-covered up jealousy and the chances are that we'll find out that the jealousy began over one incident with one individual(s) sometime in the past.

As we continue to dig beneath the surface, we will discover that our jealousy is just a manifestation of the fact that we are not getting what we want. What complicates things is that our dissatisfaction gets reflected off those around us, but those people are not the source of our problem anymore than the moon is the source of light. They are just reflecting on what has originated in our hearts.

Sincerely ridding our hearts of jealousy begins with taking a long, hard look in the mirror, not across the street or the aisle. Our emotions focused on somebody else fan the flame of jealousy and focusing on our hearts begins the process of overcoming or quenching the spirit of jealousy.

We must intentionally isolate the root of the problem, and then the rest is simple.

Not easy but simple! Let us take all our anxiety, frustration, concern, failures, setbacks, injustice, and discontent to the ONLY one who can do anything about it, **God**! Let God know that you know He could have done better by you! Pile it all on God! He is big enough to handle it all; yours, mine, and the requests of the whole universe. Tell God He owes you?

Now, if we feel and find it a bit daunting to tell God or accuse Him of owing us something, then we are on the verge of our breakthrough. The New Testament tells us that we were goners, hopelessly separated from God. But God had mercy and gave us exactly what we did not deserve: Forgiveness. The price? His Son. The truth is we owed God a debt we could not pay so God paid it, thereby erasing forever the possibility of Him owing us anything.

So, our disappointment with not getting what we want or believe we deserve pales in significance to the fact that we have been given what we needed the most. In the shadow of the cross, it is clear that God does not owe us anything. We instead owe God everything, including an apology. An apology for holding God to a debt He did not owe, a debt we held against Him but failed to recognize in the confusion and whirlwind of emotions that accompany jealousy.

God's unconditional acceptance and grace are the very reason we can bring all our disappointments and dissatisfactions to God with boldness. Again, nothing is too 'small'. We do not have to qualify and explain or feel guilty for how we feel:

> "Let us then approach God's throne of grace with confidence so that we may receive mercy and find grace to help us in time of need." Hebrew 4:16.

When we come to God with our disappointments and discontentment, we will find mercy and grace. Why? The bible says,

> "For we do not have a high priest who is unable to empathize with our weaknesses, but we have ONE who has been tempted in every way, just as we are–yet he did not sin. Hebrew 4:15".

Brethren, when we bring our wishes and wants, our dreams and disappointments to God, we are bringing them to the ONLY one who can empathize with us. We have a savior who was touched with the same emotions that leave us wondering if we can make it through. So, we must come to God's throne unapologetically, boldly, and lay our burden down at the feet of the only One who can do anything about it. Amen. That is just the beginning. Once we have wrestled our jealous spirit down internally, there is something we can do externally- a new habit – to keep us in check!

Celebration!

With Guilt, the antidote is to exercise confession, with anger, the antidote is forgiveness, while the antidote to greed is generosity. So, with jealousy- the antidote is – *Celebration*.

To guard our hearts against jealousy, we must celebrate the success and achievements of those we tend to envy! We need to go out of our way to verbally express our congratulations on their accomplishments. This must become a habit. Celebrating the success of those we tend to envy, will allow us to conquer those emotions that have the potential to drive a wedge in our relationships.

There are times when our feelings get in the way, celebrate with them anyway. This is not a suggestion to be insincere. Does that dress look good on that person? Then say it, tell them. Do you like your co-worker's car? Tell them.

Telling someone they did a great job. Wishing you could do the same is not being insincere but being honest! However, if my co-worker is good at what he does and I am not able to bring myself to complement them, then that is a problem. If our business partner builds the house

Habit #4- Confronting Jealousy

of your dreams, tell them. After all, it is true. Expressing the truth helps to free us from the emotional bondage that is such an integral part of jealousy. When we hear that someone else in your workplace gets a promotion, walk up to them and say congratulations. By doing this, we are refusing to allow dangerous emotions to control our behavior and we are protecting our hearts.

We are saying no to jealousy. It is much easier to behave our way into a new way of thinking than to think our way into a new way of behaving. We must not wait until we feel like celebrating; celebrate until you feel like it. Ridding our hearts of the destructive forces of jealousy is imperative and vital to living a free life, and it involves refusing to be taken prisoner by emotions that do not reflect reality.

Here are some foods for thought: Whose successes have we refused or were hesitant to celebrate? Who deserves a part on the back, a letter, a phone call, or a hug? Whose progress have we mentally chalked up to luck and therefore refuse to acknowledge? Whose achievements have brought to the surface some insecurity in us? Insecurity or low self-esteem has caused us to shy away from celebrating the achievements and successes of others. So instead of saying nothing or being critical, we must be intentional to develop new habits and publicly celebrate the success of others. And when that person's success has the potential to reflect negatively on us, celebrate it even more. This habit will slay the spirit of jealousy!

Lust and Lusting

> "Watch over your heart with all diligence, for from it flows the springs of life" Proverbs 4:23.

The wisest man who ever lived, King Solomon, tells us to pay attention to what is going on in our hearts because we all live from our hearts and the health of our hearts will reflect on the quality of our lives generally. Hence, we cannot afford not to talk about lust. No discussion of the heart will be complete without a word about lust. There is an assumption that men are the only victims of this heart issue. That is wrong. Most males would indeed be happy to double their quotient of guilt, anger, greed, and jealousy if it meant they could be free of the lust that runs rampant in their hearts. If it were possible to arrange a four-for-one trade, a lot of men would make a trade in a heartbeat and most wives would be happy to broker the deal for their husbands.

It seems that lust is often to blame for at least three of the four heart disorders. Sexual sin leads to guilt, for example, and sexual sins always lead to anger and betrayal.

Lust can fuel jealousy but there is another correlation between lust and our archenemies: guilt, anger, greed, and jealousy! Lust is different from guilt, anger, greed, and jealousy in one very important way; God created all our emotions, He created them, and he declared them good.

When God created Adam and Eve, He also created the concept of "one" flesh. Every indication was for Adam to strongly desire Eve and Eve to also desire Adam.

So, with sex came lust. My beloved, it was a package deal "buy one, buy all". All sales are final, with no return, no exchange, and no refunds. Lust can be a good thing because if it were not for lust; none of us probably would have been born and only a few of us would have gotten married. In a healthy marriage, lust is very alive, well, and focused.

While guilt, greed, and jealousy are always signs of trouble, it's not that obvious with lust. Lust can work for you or against you. So, before sin, there was lust, but as far as I can tell, greed, anger, guilt, and jealousy, did not show up until moments before the fall of mankind. Interestingly, all four were part of the story of our fall. And when sin entered the world, everything was corrupted, including lust.

The other thing that's different about lust is that it is an appetite. It is not going away, no matter how spiritual or committed you are. Lust is not a problem you solve; it is an appetite you manage or master so to say. So, with self-control, lust can be focused on but not eliminated. You can deal with anger and guilt once and for all but not 'lust', it is a formidable force we must reckon with, and it is here to stay for the duration.

When lust becomes problematic, it is almost always a manifestation of one or more of the heart problems we have already talked about. Clean out the anger, greed, and jealousy, and lust will invariably become much more manageable. Deal with the big four, and your ability to exercise self-control in the arena of your ability will increase dramatically.

Anger and guilt fuel sexual sin. Statistics show that some men who have had a serious pornography addiction also had unresolved issues with their fathers. 'He is just mad at his dad, really mad'. However, as we can imagine, these men saw no correlation between their unresolved anger and their uncontrollable lust. But there truly is a strong correlation.

Pornography offers a substitute for intimacy, the very thing every man needs from his earthly and heavenly father. Women are not exempt from this: sexually promiscuous women usually have secrets and hurt that date back to childhood.

Move past the issue normally associated with lust and we will find a diseased heart. A heart lined with anger, guilt, and even jealousy, with very few exemptions. Simply put, guilt, anger, greed, and jealousy weaken our resolve against sexual temptation.

Apostle Paul said in Ephesians:

> "In your anger do not sin, do not let the sun go down while you are still angry, and do not give the devil a foothold"

We can see that unresolved anger gives the devil a base of operation in our lives. But a base to do what? Whatever he desires. The options are clear: Deal with your anger and you take away the enemy's foothold; refuse to deal with it and we must prepare for the worst.

Unresolved anger serves as an avenue through which Satan gains access to any part of our lives and he is smart enough to know that nothing wreaks havoc on the human soul like sexual sin. Nothing destroys an individual's capacity for intimacy like sexual impurity. So, Satan leverages our anger for his ends, and in the end, we pay more than we are willing to pay, go further than we are willing to go, and stay longer than we are willing to stay. Anger always distorts our thinking and makes us more vulnerable to temptations. It distorts our decision-making ability. Remember, when we are angry, it is because we have convinced ourselves that somebody 'owes' us something.

Anger desensitizes us to the harm we are inflicting on others when we choose to do whatever we want. What is true of anger is also true of guilt, greed, and jealousy: All four problems reduce our resolve against sexual temptation. They tilt us off balance emotionally, leaving us vulnerable to lust. They are like out-of-control viruses weakening our spiritual and moral immune systems.

Niche or Ditch?

Must lust be ignored or chalked up to symptoms that we cannot help? No! Lust must be contained and properly focused. We will always need self-control, regardless of how healthy our hearts become. Simply put, our battle for sexual purity must be waged on several fronts and a healthy heart puts us in a stronger position to ward off temptations of all kinds. Paul told us "If we live in the Spirit, we must walk in the Spirit", by forming a habit of confession, forgiveness, celebration, and giving (talent, time, and treasures). These will help strengthen our resolve and remove the enemy's base of operation from our lives.

The healthier our hearts, the easier it will be for us to keep this God-given appetite called lust properly focused and under control. We can do this by emulating some habits namely:

(A) Confession
(B) Forgiving
(C) Giving
(D) Celebration

These are habits that will change everything. Once these four routines define the rhythm of our hearts, life will be noticeably different. Because these four habits empower us to settle our outstanding debt with God, other people, and even ourselves, removing the debt-to-debtor dynamic from the relationship paves the way to better communication, understanding, and openness:

- Confession allows us to come out from hiding.
- Forgiveness allows others to come out from the shadows.
- Generosity allows us to partner with God as he shows himself in tangible ways to the world around us.
- Celebration makes us a vehicle through which God communicates his pleasure.

That is what we were created for, and that is why these habits have the potential to change so much about our lives. Nothing goes untouched. These four habits set us free to love as God intended for us to love. Anger, greed, guilt, and jealousy are the antithesis of love. If these four monsters grow unchecked in our hearts, our efforts to love will be short-lived and thwarted. No amount of effort on our part can compensate. The purest of motives will not prevail. We cannot love while harboring one or more of these enemies because, in the end, they will overcome or overpower us.

Apostle Paul said,

> "Love is patient, love is kind, it does not boast, and it is not proud. It does not

> dishonor others, it is not self-seeking, it is not easily angered, and it keeps no record of wrongs. Love does not delight in evil but rejoices with the truth. It always protects, always trusts, always hopes, always persevere." 1 Corinthians 13:4-7.

Angry people are not patient people, guilty people are not kind, jealous people are full of envy, and greedy people cannot help but boast. Anger makes us rude; greed tempts us to be self-seeking; jealousy thrives on score-keeping, and greedy people are self-protecting. Guilt keeps us from trusting others because we have proved to be untrustworthy ourselves. The good news is that we have been commanded to love one another:

> "A new command I give you: Love one another as I have loved you, so you must love one another". John 13:34.

None of us can embrace this command with a heart tainted by even one of the four heart diseases. This means until we deal with anger, guilt, greed, and jealousy, we cannot obey the single most important command issued by our Lord and Savior Jesus Christ.

But once confessions, forgiveness, generous giving, and celebrating others become our second nature or natural default, then and only then will we be free to express

Habit #4- Confronting Jealousy

and experience the most powerful force the human soul has ever encountered: unconditional love. Just imagine, if we were all equally committed to scrubbing our hearts clean. If we made up our minds to never let the sun set on our anger, our greed, our jealousy, our guilt. What if we all guard our hearts with the same diligence, we use to guard our homes? After all, we know, have seen, and have experienced what happens when our hearts go unattended.

We have all felt the aftershock of anger, guilt, greed, and jealousy. We must wake up every day of life with an eye on the gauges of our hearts. Better yet, imagine a generation of children who grow up attuned not only to what is happening around them but inside of them as well. Imagine our children growing up with an extraordinary sensitivity to the rhythms of their hearts. It sure will make a huge difference in our society.

Now you and I have the golden opportunity to do for our children and grandchildren what perhaps our parents did not know how to do for us. As adults, we have been instructed to guard our hearts with all diligence. As parents, we have been allowed to teach our children to guard their hearts.

If the heart of a child is important to us, then we must ask them regularly about what is going on there. Then by the power of the Holy Spirit, we will be able to discern opportunities to teach them to confess, forgive, give generously, and celebrate the success of others. As they grow up, these habits will keep their hearts free from the clutters of pain and hate. These habits will enable them to develop healthy adult relationships with us in the future.

Jesus said,

> "Except your righteousness shall exceed the righteousness of the scribes and the Pharisees, ye shall in no case enter into the kingdom of heaven. Matthew 5:20".

The characteristic of the children of God is not that we do good things but that we have good motives because we are made good by the supernatural grace of God. The only thing that exceeds doing right is being-right.

Jesus came to put into any man who would let Him a new behavior, which would exceed the righteousness of the scribes and the Pharisees. Jesus said, if we are His, we must be right not only in our living but in our motives, our dreams, and the recesses of our minds. We must be pure in our motives so that God Almighty sees nothing to censure. On that day, we can stand in the eternal light of God and have nothing for God to cut out. Jesus can input His disposition into any man and make that man as unsullied and as simple as a child.

The purity which God demands is impossible unless we are remade within, **born again**. This is what Jesus has undertaken by His redemption. No man can make himself pure by obeying laws. Jesus doesn't give us rules and regulations, so this command is the truth that can only be interpreted by the disposition He alone puts in us. The great marvel of Christ's Salvation is that He alters Heredity. He does not alter our human nature; Christ alters its mainspring. Our spiritual DNA. Amen.

Chapter fifteen

Charity Begins at Home

Where do we go from here? We must start with ourselves. Ask the following people in our lives, those who know us best, about the outward expressions of what goes on in our hearts daily. They know exactly where we each should start.

Below are some starter questions:

- Do you think I struggle with being completely open about things?
- Do you feel like I have a wall?
- Do you ever feel like you are competing with me or my stuff?
- Do you feel like I compare you to other women/men/children?
- Are you ever afraid to talk to me?
- Do you ever wonder which version of me you are coming home to?

Chances are, they already know us and we also already know how they might answer some of these questions if we decide to ask. More importantly, we must decide ahead of time that we are not going to defend 'ourselves' otherwise the aim will be defeated.

Also, we must approach this prayerfully! Like a doctor whose skilled hands poke and probe until they find a sensitive spot, so God's divine truth has a way of finding its mark in our 'diseased heart' but none of that can happen until we give God access to those sensitive, otherwise 'off-limit' areas of our lives. If we do, what usually starts as threatening and uncomfortable revelations may result in the Freedom we never knew existed! I dare you to give it a try, today.

Amen.

EPILOGUE

How to be born again!

"If you openly declare that Jesus is Lord and believe in your heart that God raised him from the dead, you will be saved. For it is by believing in your heart that you are made right with God, and it is by openly declaring your faith that you are saved." Romans 10:9-10. (NLT)

- Recognize that you have sinned against God by the choices you have made
- Confess your sins to God and ask for His forgiveness
- Then forgive all those who have offended you
- Ask the Lord to pour out his spirit upon you so that you will be empowered to live for him
- Ask the Lord Jesus to be Lord and Master of your life
- Be baptized in water

- Commit to a Bible Believing Church where you can grow.

If you are already born again but struggling with these four monsters,

- Own up your culpability and ask the Lord to cleanse.
- Follow the recommended steps outlined in this book
- Look for a spiritual mentor you can be accountable to

It will be my pleasure to hear from you how this book has been a blessing to you and your testimony. Please send your comments, questions, and enquiries to:

Email address
Tel No.

God bless you.

Bose Ebhamen

About the Author

*B*ose Ebhamen is a Pastor, Family Counselor, NFPT Certified Personal Trainer, Registered Nurse and Entrepreneur.

Having migrated to the United States in the early 1990s, she has held several positions of authority in the healthcare sector and in the business community that has given her the privilege of seeing individuals struggle with the problem of guilt and shame and how it has the propensity of hindering one from becoming the best he/she can be.

Drawing inspiration from her own personal experience, she counsels and guides young people and aspiring leaders to overcome their dysfunctional backgrounds in order to soar high in life.

A graduate of the R.Trichology Academy and International Christian College and Seminary, Bose is one of the foremost deliverance ministers of our generation.

She is a director of the Reconciliation Ministries based in Houston, Texas and Columbus Indiana and she is blessed with 5 children and 5 grandchildren.

CPSIA information can be obtained
at www.ICGtesting.com
Printed in the USA
BVHW031427010922
646065BV00009B/233

9 781662 853777